RABINDRANATH TAGORE

Convalescence and Selected Songs

Mohit Chakrabarti

ATLANTIC
PUBLISHERS & DISTRIBUTORS (P) LTD

Published by

ATLANTIC

PUBLISHERS & DISTRIBUTORS (P) LTD

B-2, Vishal Enclave, Opp. Rajouri Garden,
New Delhi-110027
Phones : +91-11-25413460, 25429987, 25466842

Sales Office
7/22, Ansari Road, Darya Ganj,
New Delhi-110002
Phones : +91-11-23273880, 23275880, 23280451
Fax : +91-11-23285873
web : www.atlanticbooks.com
e-mail : info@atlanticbooks.com

Branch Office
5, Nallathambi Street, Wallajah Road,
Chennai-600002
Phones : +91-44-64611085, 32413319
e-mail : chennai@atlanticbooks.com

ISBN 978-81-7156-614-3

Printed in India
at Mehra Offset Printers, New Delhi

Dedicated to

SUSMITA DASGUPTA

PREFACE

In *Convalescence* (*Arogya*), Rabindranath Tagore reaches the zenith of perfection as a seer and poet. The ideas and concepts revealed here are pregnant with chiselled expressions of excellence and ascent of man.

Life seen at a distance and seen objectively from an unending veil of the sea of experiences is what *Arogya* endearingly represents. Significantly, the poet is beyond the worries of a murky world. His impassioned thoughts arrive at a stage where transcendence and transvaluation of values are incomparably synchronized. Prior to crossing the bar, the poet thus foresees his farewell to earth in the crystallized vision of the All Serene. The journey to Eternity paves the prized avenue of unison with the Ever Beautiful by gratefully acknowledging the beautiful world of our very own. What a preparation in poignance!

Is *Convalescence* Tagore's unparalleled gift to the marooned and macabre humanity? Perhaps so, for a look within and for a look in particular for self-analysis and self-assessment are appallingly absent. Whither introspection, whither the perfume of promises pure and perfect?

The songs of Tagore are an endless ocean of serenity and poignance. The selected songs welcome the reader to enjoy and appreciate the Tagorean world of music.

I am indebted to professor Somendranath Bandyopadhyay, Santiniketan for his affectionate suggestions.

I would also like to express my deep sense of gratitude to Dr. K.R. Gupta, Managing Director, Atlantic Publishers and Distributors, for publication of this book.

To read the poems and songs of Tagore is to be in tune with the celestial master-mind. If the book serves this purpose and evokes the ardent entry of every revered reader into the cathedral of consciousness, I would consider myself lovingly complimented.

MOHIT CHAKRABARTI

(1)

E dyulok madhumoy, madhumoy prithivir dhuli
Antare niyechhi ami tuli
Ei mahamantrakhani
Charitartha jeevaner vani.
Dine dine peyechhinu satyer ja kichhu upahar
Madhurase kshay nai tar.
Tai ei mantravani mrityur sesher prante vaje
Sav kshati mithya kari ananter ananda viraje.
Sesh sparsha nie javo jave dharanir
Vale javo tomar dhulir
Tilak parechhi bhale,
Dekhechhi nityer jyotir duryoger mayar arale.
Satyer anandarup e dhulite niyechhe murati
Ei jene e dhulay rakhinu pranati.

Pleasant is this heaven, pleasant is the earth's dust,
Upon my heart have I recast
This great vow
The message of life did bestow.
Day by day the gifts of truth did I receive whatsoever
Decay in the pleasant juicy form will ne'er favour
This message of vow on the edge of death so creates
The joy of the endless makes all loss futile and permeates.
When I shall depart with the last touch of the earth
I shall say the dust from my path
Has adorned my forehead
The halo of the Eternal have I seen in the mystery of dismay shrouded
The joyous form of Truth in this dust has taken the image,
Knowing this, I salute the dust on the earth's stage.

☆☆☆

(2)

Param sundar
Aloker snanpunya prate
Asim arup
Rupe rupe sparsamani
Rasamurti karichhe rachana,
Pratidin
Chiranutaner abhisek
Chirapuratan veditale.
Miliya shyamale nilimay
Dharanir uttariya
Vune chale chhayate alote.
Akaser hritspandan
Pallave pallave dey dola.
Prabhater kantha hate manihar kare jhilimili
Van hate vane.
Pakhider akaran gaan
Sadhuvad dite thake jeevanlakshmire.
Sav-kichhu sathe mishe manuser pritir paras
Amriter artha dey tare,
Madhumoy kare dey dharanir dhuli,
Sarvatra vichhaye dey chiramanaver singhasan.

The most beautiful
Is adorned in the holy morning
Of the bathing of light
The unending formless
With the touchstone of infinite forms
Is creating images of appreciation,
Everyday
The welcome of the ever new
At the altar of the ever old.
With unison of the green and the blue firmament
The scarf of the earth
In light and shade goes a-weaving.

The heartbeat of the sky
Does throb from leaf to leaf.
The morning's necklace sparkles
From forest to forest.
The unaccountable songs of birds
Go on thanking the goddess of the affluence of life.
The touch of human love
Does bring forth the meaning of nectar in fusion with all,
Turns the dust of the earth pleasant
And spreads the throne for the Eternal Man everywhere.

☆☆☆

(3)

Nirjan rogir ghar.
Khola dwar diye
Vanka chhaya parechhe sajyay.
Siter madhyanha tape tandratur vela
Chalechhe manthargati
Saivale durvalsrot nadir matan.
Majhe majhe jage jena dur atiter dirghaswas
Sasyahin mathe.

Mane pare katadin
Bhanga pari-tale padma
Karmahin proura prabhater
Chhayate alote
Amar udas chinta dey bhasaiya
Phenay phenay.
Sparsa kari sunyer kinara
Jeledingi chale pal tule,
Yuthabhrasta subhra megh pare thake akaser kone.
Alote jhikiya-otha ghat kankhe pallimeyeder
Ghomtay gunthita alape
Gunjarita vanka pathe amravanachchhaye
Kokil kothay dake kshane kshane nibhrita sakhay,
Chhayay kunthita pallijeevanyatrar
Rahasyer avaran kanpaiya tole mor mane.
Pukurer dhare dhare sarshekhete purna haye jaay
Dharanir pratidan roudrer daner,
Suryer mandirtale pusper naivedya thake pata.

Ami santa dristi meli nibhrita prahare
Pathayechhi nihsavda vandana,
Sei savitare jar jyotirupe pratham manush
Martyer prangantale devatar dekhechhe swarup.
Mane mane bhaviyachhi prachin yuger
Vaidik mantrer vani kanthe yadi thakita amar
Milita amar stav swachchha ei aloke aloke.

Bhasha nai bhasha nai;
Cheye dur diganter pane
Mouna more meliyachhi pandunil madhyanha-akase.

The lonely room of the patient.
Thro' open doors
The curved shadow lies prostrated on the bed.
The drowsy hours of winter with the heat of noon
Slowly trek on.
Like a river with current weak in moss.
Oft, as if, permeates the sigh of the distant past
In cropless fields.
I remember how long
The *Padma* under the broken banks
In shade and light
Of jobless middle-aged morning
Does make my aimless thoughts floating
In foams and foams.
Touching the edge of the oblivion
The fishing-boats go a-sailing
In the corner of the sky does lie the white cloud companionless.
In the sparkling pitchers on the waists of rural girls
In their closeted conversations under head-coverings
In humming zigzag avenues under the shadow of mango-groves
The cuckoo coos at times in lone branches, O where,
The rural mode of life ashamed of shade
Trembles on the veil of mystery in my mind.
The pond-sides puff up with crops of mustard seedlings
The gift of the sun with the earth's return,
The flowery offerings are placed at the temple of the sun.
In lonely hours do I spread my quiet sight
I have sent my silent salutation
To the sun with whose light the first man
On the altar of the earth has seen the image of God.
I've thought aside
If the message of the Vedic hymn of the past
My voice would adorn,
The chanting of mine would in this light unite.
No language do I have, no language, indeed;
Looking at the distant horizon
I've spread my silence in the faded blue of the sky at noon.

☆☆☆

(4)

Ghanta vaje dure.
Saharer abhrabhedi atmaghosanar
Mukharata mon theke lupta haye gelo,
Atapta magher roudre akarane chhabi elo chokhe
Jeevanyatrar prante chhilo jaha anatigochar.

Gramguli genthe genthe metho path gechhe dur-pane
Nadir parir par diye.
Prachin asathatala,
Kheyar asay lok vase
Pase rakhi hater pasara.
Ganjer tiner chalaghare
Gurer kalas sari sari,
Chete jay ghranlubdha parar kukur,
Bhir kare machhi.
Rastay upurmukhe gari,
Pater vojhai bhara,
Eke eke vasta tene uchcha sware chalechhe ojan
Arater anginay.
Vandha-khola valadera
Rastar savuj prante ghas kheye phere,
Lejer chamar hane pithe.
Sarse achhe stupakar
Golay tolar apekshay.
Jelenouko elo ghate,
Jhuri kankhe jutechhe mechhuni;
Mathar upare ore chil.
Mahajani noukogulo dhalutate vandha pasapasi.
Malla vunitechhe jal roudre vasi chaler upare.
Ankari mosher gala santariya chashi bhese chale
Opare dhaner khete
Adure vaner urdhe mandirer chura
Jhalichhe prabhat-roudraloke.
Mather adrisya pare chale relgari

Kshina hate kshinatar
Dhwanirekha tene diye vataser vuke,
Paschate dhonyay meli
Duratva-jayer dirgha vijaypataka.

Mane elo, kichhui se nay, sei vahudin age
Dupahar rati,
Nouka vandha gangar kinare.
Jyotsnay chikkan jal,
Ghanibhuta chhayamurti nishkampa aranya-tire-tire,
Kvachit vaner phanke dekha jay pradiper sikha.
Sahasa uthinu jege.
Savdasunya nisitha-akase
Uthichhe ganer dhwani tarun kanther,
Chhutichhe bhantir srote tanvi nouka tartar vege.
Muhurte adrisya haye gelo;
Dui pare stavdha vane jagiya rahila siharan;
Chander-mukut-para achanchal ratrir pratima
Rahila nirvak haye parabhuta ghumer asane.

Paschimer gangatir, saharer seshprante vasa.
Dur prasarita char
Sunya akaser niche sunyatar bhashya kare jena.
Hetha hotha chare goru sasyasesh vajrar khete;
Tarmujer lata hate
Chhagal khedaye rakhe kathi hate krishan-valak.
Kothao va eka pallinari
Saker sandhane phere jhuri niye kankhe.
Kabhu vahu dure chale nadir rekhar pase pase
Nataprishtha klishtagati guntana malla ek sari.
Jale sthale sajiver ar chinha nai saravela.
Golak-chanpar gachh anadrita kachher vagane;
Talay-asan-gantha vriddha mahanim
Nivir gambhir tar abhijatyachhaya.
Ratre setha vaker asray.
Indaray tana jal
Nala veye saradin kulu kulu chale
Bhuttar phasale dite pran.
Bhajiya jantay bhange gam
Pital-kankan-para hate.
Madhyanha avishta kare ektana sur.

Pathe-chala ei dekhasona
Chhila jaha kshanachar
Chetanar pratyanta pradese,
Chitte aj tai jege othe;
Ei sav upekshita chhavi
Jeevaner sarvasesh vichchhedvedana
Durer ghantar rave ene dey mane.

At a distance, the bell rings.
The clamorous self-announcement piercing the sky of the
town
From the mind disappeared
In the heated sun of *Magh*, flashed in the eyes
without reason the picture
That on the edge`of the way of life not very visible remained.
Knitting the hamlets the meadowy path has towards
the distance gone
Crossing o'er the embankments of the river.
The ancient shade of the *Asatha* tree,
The people are seated in the hope of crossing the river
Keeping the marketing products nearby.
In the tinplate rooms of the *gunj*
Files of pictures with condensed juice of sugar-candies.
The dogs of the locality lick by being a prey to perfume.

Flies crowd.
On the roads, carts put upside down
Are burdened with jute
Weighing goes on aloud by pulling the bags one by one
In the courtyard of the storehouse.
The oxen bereft of yokes
Squander on the green edge of the road by eating grass,
Beat on the back by the hairy fan on the tail.
Heaps of mustard are there
Waiting for storage in the corn-containers.
The fishing boats come on the banks,
The fisherwomen have assembled with buckets on their
waists:
Overhead the kite flies.
The business-boats are bound side by side on the sloping
sandbanks.

Sitting in the sun, the oarsmen are weaving nets on the
roof of tin sheds
The ploughman floats on swimming by clasping the neck of
the buffalo
Towards the other side in paddy fields.
Beyond the forest, the apex of the temple not far away
Is shining in the morning sunlight.
Beyond the visible side of the field, the train runs on
With gradually feeble
Whistling lines of sound drawn on the canvas of ether
Spreading the smoke behind —
As a mark of the long flag of victory of winning the distance.
I remember that's nothing, long long ago.
It was midnight.
The boats were anchored on the bank of the Ganges
The shining water in moonlight.
The images of shadow consolidated on the edges of the
forest untrembled
The flame of the lamp is rarely seen thro' the forest.
Suddenly I awoke.
In the soundless midnight sky
The young voice in the song echoes,
The lean boat sweepingly runs in the ebb-tide current
In an instant it vanished:
Mystery reigned in the sombre forest on the two banks:
The image of the quiet night dressed with the crown
of the moon
In the seat of the humbled slumber did speechless remain.
The western bank of the Ganges, the residence is at the
fag-end of the town.
The long stretched sand bank
Beneath the vacant sky as if makes a commentary on futility.
Cows graze to and fro in the empty field of maize,
From the creepers of water-melon
The farmer-boy drives with a stick the goats away.
Somewhere, again, the rural woman
Roams in search of spinach with a basket on her waist.
Oft beside the river-line far away
A group of oarsmen with bowed down backs, tired movements,
pulling the ropes.

No more freshness prevails in the water of land all day long.
In the nearby garden, the *golakchanpa* is unendeared
The old great *neem* tree with seat prepared below
The aristocratic shadow of hers deep and serene.
Storks take shelter at night there.
The water pulled out of the well
All day long makes rippling sounds in its course through
the drains
To instil life in the fields of oats.
Bhajiya crushes wheat in a wheel-crusher
With her brass-bangled hands
The stretched tune the noon enchants.

This on-the-way scene
Transitory as it was
In the distant domain of consciousness,
Up that comes in the mind today.
All these pictures discarded
The latest pain of separation of life
Bring forth in the mind with the sound of the distant bell.

☆☆☆

(5)

Mukta vatayanprante janasunya ghare
Vase thaki nistavdha prahare,
Vahire shyamal chhande uthe gaan
Dharanir praner ahavan.
Amriter utsasrote
Chitta bhese chale jay diganter nilim alote.
Kar pane pathaive stuti
Vyagra ei maner akuti,
Amulyere mulya dite phire se khunjiya vanirup,
Kare thake chup,
Vale, ami anandita, chhanda jay thami,
Vale, dhanya ami.

On the edge of the open window, in the lonely parlour
I remain seated in the silent hour.
Outside in rhythm of the green songs herald
The beckonings of the life of the world.
Towards the flow of the origin of eternity
The mind floats in with the horizon's bluish spree.
To whom adoration is to be sent
Is the eager mind's only incumbent,
On he seeks in the image of words the priceless to pay,
Not a word does he say.
Glad am I, he murmurs, rhythm comes to a stop,
Says he, the harvest of thanks I crop.

☆ ☆ ☆

(6)

Ati dure akaser sukumar pandur nilima
Aranya tahari tale urdhve vahu meli
Apan shyamal arghya nihsavde karichhe nivedan.
Magher turun roudra dharanir pare
Vichhaila dike dike syachchha aloker uttariya.
E katha rakhinu likhe
Udasin chitrakar ei chhavi muchhivar age.

The pale fine firmament is in the great distance
The forest stretches its long arm overhead beneath her
And silently does submit its own green offerings.
The young sun of *Magh* on earth
Spreads everywhere the scarf of transparent light.
This had I put in writing
Ere the stoical artist erased this picture.

☆☆☆

(7)

Hingsra ratri ase chupe chupe
Gata val sarirer sithil argal bhenge diye
Antare pravesh kare,
Haran karite thake jeevaner gouraver rup.
Kalimar akramane har mane mon.
E parabhaver lajja e avasader apaman
Jakhan ghaniye othe sahasa digante dekha dey
Diner patakakhani svarnakiraner rekha-anka;
Akaser jena kon dur kendra hate
Uthe dhvani mithya mithya vali.
Prabhater prasanna aloke
Duhkhavijayeer murti dekhi apanar
Jirnadeha-durger sikhare.

Silently comes the ferocious night
Breaking the flexible bars of body *sans* strength
Enters the heart,
Goes on stealing the glorious *mien* of life.
The mind does accept defeat at the hands of humiliation.
When the shame of this defeat, the disgrace of boredom
Darkens, suddenly in the horizon is seen
The flag of the day painted with the light of gold.
From the distant centre what a sound, as it were,
Arises to declare it false, utterly false.
In the pleasing light of the morn
I behold the image of myself, the winner of sorrow
On the peak of the fort of the worn-out body.

☆☆☆

(8)

Eka vase sangsarer pranta-janalay
Diganter nilimay chokhe pare ananter bhasha.
Alo ase chhayay jarita
Sirisher gachh hate shyamaler snigdha sakhya vahi.
Vaje mane — nahe dur, nahe vahu dur.
Patharekha lin hala astagirisikhar-arale.
Stavdha ami dinanter panthasala-dware,
Dure dipti dey kshane kshane
Sesh tirtha-mandirer chura.
Setha singhadware vaje din-avasaner ragini
Jar murchhanay mesa e janmer ja-kichhu sundar,
Sparsa ja karechhe pran dirgha jatrapathe
Purnatar ingit janaye.
Vaje mane — nahe dur, nahe vahu dur.

Sitting alone beside the edged window of the world
The eyes encounter the language of the endless in the
horizon of the sky.
Embraced in shadow does the light come
Carrying the smooth friendship of the green from the
Sirish tree.
In the mind rings: not far, not very far.
The line of the avenue merged in the backdrop of the
peak of the setting mountain,
Silent am I beside the door of the inn of the day's end,
In the distance, at times, lustre spreads
The peak of the last pilgrim-temple.
There at the entrance-door the *ragini* of the day's
end plays on.
With whose resonance whatever is beautiful in this life,
Whatever touches the heart in its long journey
Is merged with beckonings of fulness.
In the mind rings: not far, not very far.

☆☆☆

(9)

Virat sristir kshetre
Atasvajir khela akase akase
Surya tara laye
Jug-juganter parimape.
Anadi adrisya hate amio esechhi
Kshudra agnikana niye
Ek prante kshudra dese kale.
Prasthaner anke aj esechhi jemani
Dipsikha mlan haye ela,
Chhayate parila dhara e khelar mayar swarup,
Slath haye ela dhire
Sukh duhkha natyasajyaguli.
Dekhilam, juge juge natnati vahu sata sata
Phele gechhe nanaranga ves tahader
Rangasala-dwarer vahire.
Dekhilam chahi
Sata sata nirvapita nakshatrer nepathyaprangane
Nataraj nistavadha ekaki.

Amid the vast creation
The game of fireworks throughout the sky
Goes on along with the sun and the stars
In the yardstick of age beyond age.
I have also come from the endless and the invisible
With a trifling splinter of fire
At one end in a small space and time.
Come as I have today in the act of departure,
The flame of the lamp turned pale.
The reality of enchantment of this play is revealed
in shadow.
Slowly the dramatic costumes
Of happiness and sorrow become loose.
I saw from time to time players in legion

Have left their variegated dresses
Outside the door of the theatre.
I saw:
In the 'drop of hundreds of switched-off stars
The silent and lone *Nataraj*.

☆☆☆

(10)

Alas samaydhara veye
Mon chale sunya-pane cheye.
Se mahasunyer pathe chhaya-anka chhavi pare chokhe.
Kata kal dale dale gechhe kata loke
Sudirgha atite
Jayoddhvata praval gatite.
Esechhe samrajyalobhi Pathaner dal,
Esechhe Mogal,
Vijayrather chaka
Urayechhe dhulijal, uriyachhe vijaypataka.
Sunyapathe chai
Aj tar kono chihna nai.
Nirmal se nilimay prabhate o sandhay rangalo
Juge juge suryoday suryaster alo.
Arvar sei sunyatale
Asiyachhe dale dale
Louhavandha pathe
Analnisvasi rathe
Praval Engrej,
Vikirna karechhe tar tej.
Jani taro path diye vaye jave kal,
Kothay bhasaye deve samrajyer desh-vera jal.
Jani tar panyavahi sena
Jyotishkaloker pathe rekhamatra chihna rakhive na.

Matir prithivi-pane ankhi meli jave
Dekhi setha kalakalarave
Vipul janata chale
Nana pathe nana dale dale
Jug-jugantar hate manusher nitya prayojane
Jeevane marane.
Ora chirakal
Tane danr, dhare thake hal;
Ora mathe mathe

Vij vone, paka dhan kate.
Ora kaj kare
Nagare prantare.
Rajchhatra bhenge pare, ranadanka savda nahi tole,
Jayastambha murasama artha tar bhole,
Raktamakha astrahate jata rakta ankhi
Sisupathya kahinite thake mukh dhaki.
Ora kaj kare
Deshe deshantare
Anga Banga Kalinger samudra nadir ghate ghate,
Panjabe Bombai Gujarate.
Guru guru garjan gun gun swar
Dinratre gantha pari dinayatra karichhe mukhar.
Duhkha sukh divas rajani
Mandrita kariya tole jeevaner mahamantradhwani.
Sata sata samrajyer bhagnasesh-pare
Ora kaj kare.

Rowing through the flow of idle time
The mind goes on looking towards emptiness.
The picture painted in shadow arrests the eyes in the
path of that vast emptiness.
In groups, for time endless, so many people have gone
In time long past
In forceful speed of the pomp of victory.
The groups of the Pathans have come with the
greed of empire.
The Moghuls have come.
The wheels of the chariot of victory
Have sped past the web of dust and the flag of victory
Towards the avenue of emptiness do I look
No trace of that do I find today.
In that clear sky in the morn and in the eve
The light of sunrise and sunset adorned from
time to time.
Once again in that abode of emptiness
In groups have come
Thro' iron-string avenue
In the chariot that believes in fire
The mighty English
Have exposed their power.

Know I that time would flow on even in their avenue
To the endless would it sweep away the countywide
dragnet of empire.
Know I that her soldiers carrying the burden of commodities
Would leave no trace in the avenue of the world of light.

Opening eyes towards the world of earth
We see there in murmuring sounds
Endless crowd tread on
In diverse avenues and in different groups
From time beyond time in eternal human needs
In life and death.
Endlessly do they
Pull on oars, hold on the steering.
From field to field do they
Sow seeds, reap ripe paddy.
They work
In cities and fields.
The septre tumbles down, no sound emerges from the drum
of war.
The tower of victory forgets like the dunce its meaning
All the bloody eyes with bloodstained weapons in hands
Remain wrapped in stories meant for children.
They work
In countries beyond countries
In the sea-shores and river-banks of *Anga, Banga*
and *Kalinga*,
In Punjab, Bombay and Gujarat.
The roaring and the humming sounds
By day and at night are enclasped and make the passing
of the day enamoured.

Sorrow and happiness, day and night
The sounds of great chanting of life do make resonant.
On the remains of ruins of hundreds of empires
They work.

☆☆☆

(11)

Palash anandamurti jeevaner phalgoondiner
Aj ei sammanhiner
Daridravelay dile dekha
Jetha ami sathihin eka
Utsaver prangon-vahire
Sasyahin marumoy tire.
Jekhane e dharanir prafulla praner kunja hate
Anadrita din mor niruddesh srote
Chhinnavrinta chaliyachhe bhese
Vasanter seshe.
Tavuo to kripanata nai tava dane,
Jouvaner purna mulya dile mor diptihin prane.
Adrister avajnare kara ni swikar,
Ghuchaile avasad tar,
Janaile chitte mor labhi anuksan
Sundarer abhyarthana, naviner ase nimantran.

Palash is the emblem of joy of the spring of life,
Today to one bereft of honour
In his poor hours you met
Where I, the companionless, am alone
Out of the courtyard of ceremonies
On the sandy shores of the desert *sans* crops.
Where from the boisterous garden of life of this earth
My unwelcome days towards streams lost
Like torn sheets are gone afloating
At the end of the spring.

Even then, your gift is beyond austerity
The full price of youth you have offered in my heart *sans* lustre
The aversion of providence you denied not
Her tiredness you did ameliorate,
Conveyed me and so am I all the time
Prized with the welcome of Beauty, the invitation of the young.

☆☆☆

(12)

Dwar khola chhila mane, asatarke setha akasmat
Legechhila ki lagiya kotha hate duhkher aghat,
Se lajjay khule gela marmatale prachchhanna je val
Jeevaner nihita samval.
Urddhva hate jayadhwani
Antare diganta pathe namila takhani
Anander vichchhurita alo
Muhurte andhar-megh dirna kari hridaye chharalo.
Kshudra kotarer asamman
Lupta hala, nikhiler asane dekhinu nij sthan,
Anande anandamoy
Chitta mor kari nila joy,
Utsaver path
Chine nila muktikshetre sagourave apon jagat.
Duhkha-hana glani jata achhe,
Chhaya se, milalo tar kachhe.

The door of the mind was open, suddenly in unawareness
The stroke of sorrow befell there I know not from where
The shame gushed forth the unexposed strength
That embodies the inherent source of life.
The slogan of victory from above
Instantly came down in the mind thro' the path of
the horizon
The splashed light of joy
Spread in a moment in the mind, piercing the cloud of darkness
The humiliation of the tiny crevice
Was abolished, saw I my place in the seat of the world.
With joy in abundance
My mind embraced victory.
The avenue of ceremony
In glory did identify its own world in the arena of
emancipation.
The clamours arising out of sorrow
Turned into shadows and ematiated in it.

☆ ☆ ☆

(13)

Bhalobasa ekdin esechhila tarun bayase
Nirjharer pralapkallole,
Ajana sikhar hate
Sahasa vismay vahi ani,
Bhru bhangita pashaner nischal nirdesh
Langhiya uchchhal parihase,
Batasere kari dhairyahara,
Parichaydhara-majhe tarangiya aparichayer
Abhabita rahashyer bhasha
Charidike sthir jaha parimita nitya pratyasita
Tari madhye mukta kari dhavaman vidroher dhara.

Aj sei bhalobasa snigdha santwanar stavdhatay
Rayechhe nihsavda haye prachchhanna gabhire.
Chari dike nikhiler vrihat santite
Milechhe se sahaj milane,
Tapaswini rajanir tarar aloy tar alo,
Pujarata aranyer pushpa arghye tahar madhuri.

Love came once in young age
With murmurs of the fountain.
From the peak unknown
With a sudden sense of wonder
The static direction of stones curved like eyebrows
Being carried over with the overflowing frown,
Making the wind restless,
Waving amid the flow of identity
The language of unimaginable mystery of the unknown
All around whatever is static, proportionate and eternally exposed
The flow of running revolt rings with the muse of emancipation.

That love today with the silence of pleasing consolation
In the backdrop of the deep has remained soundless.

Everywhere in the vastness of peace of the world
It is in unassuming unison
Its light is with the light of the stars of the meditating
night.
Its beauty is with the flowery offerings of worship of the
night.

☆☆☆

(14)

Pratyaha prabhatkale bhakta e kukur
Stavdha haye vase thake asaner kachhe
Jatakshane sanga tar karina swikar
Karasparsa diye.
Etuku swikriti labh kari
Sarvange tarangi uthe anandapravaha.
Vakyahin pranilok-majhe
Ei jeev sudhu
Bhalo manda sav bhed kari
Dekhechhe sampurna manushere;
Dekhechhe anande jare pran deoya jay
Jare dhele deoya jay ahetuk prem,
Asim chaitanyaloke
Path dekhaiya dey jahar chetana.
Dekhi jave muk hridayer
Pranpan atmanivedan
Apanar dinata janaye,
Bhaviya na pai o je kee mulya karechhe avishkar
Apan sahajvodhe manavswarupe;
Bhashahin drishtir karun vyakulata
Vojhe jaha vojhate pare na,
Amare vujhaye dey – srishti-majhe manaver satya parichay.

This devoted dog
Every morning silently remains seated beside my seat
Until I admit his company
With the touch of my hands.
With this little recognition
The waves of joy ripple all through the body.
Amid the speechless world of animals
This creature alone
Barring all good and evil
The man *in toto* has seen.

It has seen one to whom in joy the life can be laid
Love uncalled for can be showered upon
To the unending world of consciousness,
One whose awareness the avenue shows.
When I behold the dumb heart's
Untiring self-submission,
Proclaiming the poverty of its own.
I fail to make out what price it has haunted out
With its easy feelings in the form of man.
The piteous anxieties of its speechless look
Fail to spell out whatever it feels,
It makes me understand: The real worth of man is
in the creation.

☆☆☆

(15)

Khyati ninda par haye jeevaner esechhi pradoshe
Vidayer ghate achhi vase.
Apanar dehatare asangsaye karechhi viswas,
Jarar sujog peye nijere se kare parihas,
Sakal kajei dekhi kevali ghatay viparyay,
Amar kartritya kare kshay;
Sei apaman hate vanchate jahara
Avisram ditechhe pahara,
Pashe jara danrayechhe dinanter sesh ayojane,
Nam na-i valilam tahara rahila mane mane.
Tahara diyechhe more soubhagyer sesh parichay,
Bhulaye rakhichhe tara durval praner parajay;
E katha swikar tara kare
Khyati pratipatti jata sujogya sakshamder tare;
Taharai karichhe praman
Akshamer bhagye achhe jeevaner sreshtha jei dan.
Samasta jeevan dhare khyatir khajna dite hay
Kichhu se sahena apachay,
Sav mulya phuraile je daina premer arghya ane
Asimer swakshar sekhane.

Crossing over fame and disgrace have I arrived at the
evening of life

Seated on the steps of adieu
Doubtlessly have I believed this physique of my own,
With the chance of disease it does mock at itself
See I in every activity it brings forth a disaster,
My authority does disown.
To save from that disgrace
Those who untiringly guard
Have stood beside me in the last welcome of the end of the day
Let me not disclose their names, let them remain in the mind.
They've given me the last recognition of good fortune,
They've made me forget the defeat of the frail heart

They admit
Fame and authority to the befitting and to the able belong.
Alone they prove
To the lot of the unable the best gift does await.
All through the life the price of fame is to be paid,
No wastage does it allow,
With the end of all poverty the offerings of love
does that poverty bring back,
The sign of the endless dazzles there.

☆☆☆

(16)

Din pare jay din, stavdha vase thaki
Bhavi mane jeevaner dan jata kata tar vaki
Chukaye sanchay apachay.
Ajatne kee haye gechhe kshay,
Kee peyechhi prapya jaha, kee diyechhi jaha chhila deya,
Kee rayechhe sesher patheya.
Jara kachhe esechhila jara chale giyechhila dure
Tader paraskhani raye gechhe mor mon sure.
Anyamane kare chini nai,
Vidayer padadhwani prane aj vajichhe vrithai,
Hayto hay ni jana kshama kare ke giyechhe chale
Kathati na vale.
Jadi bhul kare thaki tahar vichar
Kshobh ki rakhive tavu jakhan rava na ami ar.
Kata sutra chhinna hala jeevaner astranmay
Jora lagavare ar rave na samay.
Jeevaner seshprante je prem rayechhe niravadhi
Mor kono asamman tahe kshatachihna dey jadi
Amar mrityur hasta arogya aniya dik tare
E kathai bhavi vare vare.

Day after day wanes away, silently I remain seated,
Thinking over the gifts of life how much is left
By meeting the wastage of savings.
What is waned *sans* care,
Whate'er due I have received, whate'ver to be given I've delivered
What is left as the remnant for the end.
Those who came near, those who went far away
With what tunings of mine their touch has still remained
Whom I recognized not in absent-mindedness.
The footfalls of farewell today are ringing in the heart in vain
Perhaps I knew not who had left away forgiving me
Without speaking.

If any error do I commit, its judgment
Will you in grievance nurse when I shall be no more?
So many ties were torn, the strappings of life
No time will find to be entwined.
The love that has continually remained at the fag-end of life,
If any sign of wound is inflicted with any dishonour of mine
Let healing be brought forth with my palms of death:
This do I think time and again.

☆☆☆

(17)

Jakhan e deha hate roge o jaray
Dine dine samarthya jharay,
Jouvan e jirnaneer pichhe phele diye jay phanki
Keval saisav thake vaki.
Vandha ghare karmakshuvdha sangsar-vahire
Asakta se sisuchitta ma khunjiya phire.
Vittahara pran lubhdha hay
Vinamulye sneher prasray
Karo kachhe karivare labh
Jar abirbhav
Kshinajivitere kare dan
Jeevaner pratham samman.
'Thako tumi' mane niye eituku chaoya
Ke tare janate pare tar prati nikhiler daoya
Sudhu venche thakivar.
E vismay varvar
Aji ase prane,
Pranalakshmi-dharitrir gabhir ahavane
Ma danray ese
Je ma chirapuratan nutaner vese.

When this body with decay and disease
Strength does lose day by day
Youth slips away leaving this tattered nest
Childhood alone remains.
In the closed room outside the world of action-grieved one
The frail mind of the child its mother haunts.
The heart *sans* wealth is allured
The shelter of affection without price
To receive from someone
Whose debut
To the shortlived does offer
The first honour of life.

This much is the askance with the 'let-you-remain' mind.
Who can convey the demand of the world to Him
Only to live?
Again and again this wonder
Arrives at the heart
With the profound call of the world blessed with life
Mother comes and stands —
The mother ever old — with the dress of the new.

☆☆☆

(18)

Phasal kata hale sara math haye jay phank
Anadarer sasya gajay tuchchha damer sak.
Anchal bhare tulte ase gariv-gharer meye,
Khusi haye varite jay, ja jote tai peye.
Ajke amar chash chalena, nai langaler valai
Poro mather kunremite manthar din chalai.
Jamite ras kichhu achhe sakta jay ni anti,
Phalay na se phal tavuo savuj rakhe mati.
Sravan amar gechhe chale nai vadaler dhara,
Aghran se sonar dhaner din karechhe sara.
Chaitra amar rode pora, sukno jakhan nadi
Vuno phaler jhoper talay chhaya vichhay jadi,
Janva amar sesher mase bhagya dey ni phanki,
Shyamal dharar sange amar vandhan raila vaki.

With the reaping of harvest, the cornfield becomes vacant
The crop of neglect, the spinach, grows of value scant.
The women of the poor families come to pluck in plenty
Home they return in joy, whatever they get the bounteous pretty.
Today I fail to plough, no scope for ploughing have I
In left out cornfields' idleness, lazy days I pass by.
Life in land is somewhat there, the seed is not yet ripe,
Fruit it does not bring forth, the soil is still alive.
My *Sravan* is gone away, there's rain no more
Aghran with golden days of paddy is already o'er.
My *Chaitra* is burnt in the sun, when the river is dry
If under the bush of fruit wild its shadow does sigh
I shall know then that in my last month my lot did not slip,
My enchantment with the green world still does peep.

☆☆☆

(19)

Didimani.
Aphuran santwanar khani.
Kono klanti kono kles
Mukhe chihna dey nai les.
Kono bhay kono ghrina kono kaje kichhumatra glani
Sevar madhurye chhaya nahi dey ani.
E akhanda prasannata ghire tare rayechhe ujjwali,
Rachitechhe santir mandali;
Kshipra hastakshepe
Charidike swasti dey vyepe;
Aswaser vani sumadhur
Avasad kari dey dur.
E snehamadhuryadhara
Aksham rogire ghire apanar rachichhe kinara;
Aviram paras chintar
Vichitra phasale jena urvar karichhe din tar.
E madhurya karite sarthak
Etakhani nirvaler chhila avasyak.
Avak haiya tare dekhi,
Rogir deher majhe ananta sisure dekhechhe ki.

Didimani.
The mine of consolation unending.
No boredom no distress
Not a least does in countenance impress.
No fear, no hatred, not a least scare in any work
Shadow does bring forth in the grace of service
This gladness unhindered has luminously embraced him
And an assembly of peace is creating.
With quick grace of hands
Calmness spreads in numbness all around.
The pleasant words of assurance
Away do boredom drive
This spring of affection and grace

Controls itself by encompassing the patient *sans* strength
With thoughts of incessant touch
His days are enriched with harvest diverse.
To glorify this grace
Such a strengthless one did necessitate.
In wonder do I see her:
Has she seen the eternal child in the body of the patient?

☆☆☆

(20)

Visudada —
Dirghavapu driravahu duhsaha kartavye nahi vadha,
Vuddhite ujjwal chitta tar
Sarvadehe tatparata karichhe vistur.
Tandrar arale
Rogaklishta klanta ratrikale
Murtiman saktir jagrata rup prane
Valishtha aswas vahi ane,
Nirnimesh nakshatrer majhe
Jeman jagrata sakti nihsavda viraje
Amogh aswase
Supta ratre viswer akase.
Jakhan sudhay more duhkha ki rayechhe konokhane
Mane hay nai tar mane,
Duhkha michhe bhram
Apan pourushe tare apani kariva atikram
Sevar bhitare sakti durvaler dehe kare dan
Valer samman.

Visudada —
With big physique, stretched out arms undaunted in
unbearable deeds
Bright in intelligence is his mind
Alertness all over his body spreads
In the backdrop of drowsiness
In tired moments of nights afflicted with disease
In a heart embodied with the living form of standing strength
Brings forth powerful assurance,
Amid stars instantaneous
Alike the living force that silently heralds
In unfailing assurance
In the sky of the universe at night asleep
When he says, 'Do you feel sorrow anywhere?'
No meaning is there I think,

Sorrow is a sham illusion,
With manliness of mine shall I overcome it.
The strength inherent in service affords in the body of the weak
The honour of the strong.

☆☆☆

(21)

Chiradin achhi ami akejor dale;
Vaje lekha vaje para din kate mithya vaje chhale.
Je guni katate pare vela tar vina avasyake
Tare 'eso eso' vale jatna kare vasai vaithake.
Kejo lokder kari bhay,
Kavjite ghari vendhe sakta kare vendhechhe samay –
Vaje kharacher tare udvritta kichhui nei hate,
Amader mato kunre lajja pay tader sakshate.
Samay karite nashta amra ostad,
Kajer karite kshati nanamato pete rakhi phand.
Amar sarirta je vyestader taphate bhagay,
Apanar sakti nei paradehe masul lagay.
Sarojdadar dike chai
Sav tate raji dekhi, kajkarma jena kichhu nai,
Samayer bhandarete deoya nei chavi,
Amar matan ei akshamer davi
Metavar achhe tar akshunna udar avasar,
Dite pare akripan aklanta nirbhar.
Dwiprahar ratrivela stimita aloke
Sahasa tahar murti pare jave chokhe
Mane bhavi aswaser tari veye dut ke pathale,
Duryoger duhswapna katale.
Dayhin manusher abhavita ei avirbhav
Dayahin adristater vandisale mahamulya labh.

Eternally am I in the group of the jobless;
In trash writing and reading, my days roll on
in sham strategies,
I welcome the learned who spends his time in
unwanted mood
With care in my sitting room saying 'come, please come'.
I do fear the work-worried people
Tightly they have arrested time with watches
on their wrists

Nothing is there to spend in extravagance to an excess
Idle folk like us are ashamed of this amid them.
Masters are we to idle away time
To disrupt work in manifold ways, we lay our traps
This frame of mine does keep the busy far away
Strength have I not to surcharge others' frames.
I look at Sarojdada
He agrees at everything as if he has no work
Unlocked is the storehouse of his time,
The demands of the disabled like me
Enjoy leisure from him wide and uninterrupted
Bounteous, untiring and dependable,
At dead night in drooping light
Suddenly his image my eyes visualize
Think I aside, who sent the messenger rowing the
boat of assurance
The nightmare of adversaries did erase.
This unimagined debut of a man *sans* any assignment
Is a priceless profit in the prison-house of merciless
providence.

☆☆☆

(22)

Nagadhirajer dur nevu-nikunjer
Rasapatraguli
Anila e sajyatale
Janahin prabhater ravir mitrata,
Ajana nirjharinir
Vichchhurita alokchchhatar
Hiranmoy lipi,
Sunivir aranyavithir
Nihsavda marmare vijarita
Snigdha hridayer doutyakhani.
Rogapangu lekhanir viral bhashar
Ingite pathay kavi asirvad tar.

The juiceful containers of
The distant lemon-garden of the king of mountains
Brought at the feet of this bed
The friendship of the sun of the lovely morning
The golden writings
Of the spray of light splashed
Entangled with soundless murmurings
Of profound forest-groves
The liaison of the refreshing heart remains.
With the beckonings of the rare language of the disease-dubbed pen
The poet conveys his blessings.

☆☆☆

(23)

Nari tumi dhanya,
Achhe ghar achhe gharkanna.
Tari madhye rekhechha ektukhani phank.
Setha hate pase kane vahirer durvaler dak.
Niye esa susrushar dali,
Sneha dao dhali.
Je jeevalakshmir mane palaner sakti vahaman
Nari tumi nitya sona tahari ahavan.
Srishti-Vidhatar
Niyechha karmer bhar.
Tumi nari
Tanhari apan sahakari.
Unmukta karite thaka arogyer path,
Navin karite thaka jirna je jagat,
Srihara je tar 'pare tomar dhairyer sima nai,
Apan asadhya diye daya tava tanichhe tarai.
Vuddhibhrashta asahishnu apaman kare vare vare
Chakshu muchhe kshama kara tare.
Akritajnatar dware aghat sahichha dinrati,
Lao sir pati.
Je abhagya nahi lage kaje
Pranalakshmi phele jare avarjana-majhe
Tumi tare anichha kuraye,
Tar lanchhanar tap snigdha haste ditechha juraye.
Devatare je puja devar
Durbhagare kara dan sei mulya tomar sevar,
Viswer palani sakti nij virye vaha chupe chupe
Madhurir rupe.
Bhrashta jei bhagna jei virup vikrita
Tari lagi sundarer hater amrita.

Hail to you, woman,
A room you have and activities household.
A little space amid this you have left

The call of the weak outside reaches the ears from there.
The offerings of care do you bring along
And shower affection
The goddess of welfare at all creatures bears in mind
the strength to restore
Woman, you hear her beckonings all the time.
From the creator
You have assigned yourself
Woman, you are
His own partner
The avenues of convalescence you unfold
The world tattered you make anew
To one *sans* beauty receives your unending endurance
Your kindness adorned with own unlimited service they do enjoy.
The one bereft of reasoning and forbearance humiliates you
time and again
Forgive him by drying your eyes.
Day and night are you putting up assault at the doors of
ingratitude
With head bowed down.
The hapless with no use of service
Whom the goddess of the wealth of life into the
dustbin throws
You have brought him back picking him up
With soothing hands you are alleviating his heat of
humiliation.
The offerings meant for God
The worth of your service to the hapless you give
Silently the strength of caressing the universe you carry
with courage own
In pleasing forms.
To one ostracized, broken, hapless, deformed,
The nectar from the hands of the beautiful is for him alone.

☆☆☆

(24)

Alas sajyar pase jeevan manthargati chale,
Rache silpa saivaler dale,
Maryada naiko tar tavu tahe ray
Jeevaner swalpamulya kichhu parichay.

Slowly goes life beside the idle bed.
Artistry does create in the mossy shed.
No honour it has, yet it remains there, too,
The little worth of life, identities a few.

☆☆☆

(25)

Virat manavchitte
Akathita vanipunja
Avyakta avege phire kal hate kale
Mahasunye niharika-sama.
Se amar manahsimanar
Sahasa aghate chhinna haye
Akare hayechhe ghanibhuta,
Avartan karitechhe amar rachana-kakshapathe.

In the vast human mind
The cluster of words untold
Hovers from time to time with emotions unexpressed.
Like a nebula in the enormous oblivion.
In the arena of my mind
Suddenly being whisked away in a stroke
Consolidated has it become
And is rotating in my creative hemisphere.

☆ ☆ ☆

(26)

E katha se katha mane ase
Varshaseshe sarater megh jena phirichhe vatase.
Kajer vandhanhara sunye kare michhe anagona,
Kakhano rupali anke kakhano phutaye tole sona.
Adbhut murti se rache diganter kone
Rekhar vadal kare punah punah jena anyamane.
Vashper se silpakaj jena anander avahela,
Konokhane day nei tai tar arthahin khela.
Jagar dayitva achhe kaj niye tai othapara.
Ghumer to day nei, elomelo swapna tai gara.
Maner swapner dhat chapa thake kajer sasane,
Vasite pay na chhuti swaraj-asane.
Jemni se pay chhara kheyale kheyale kare bhir.
Swapna diye rache jena urukshu pakhir kon nir.
Apanar majhe tai petechhi praman
Swapner e paglami viswer adim upadan.
Tahare damane rakhe, dhruva kare srishtir pranali
Kartritva prachanda valasali.
Silper naipunya ei uddamere srinkhalita kara,
Adharake dhara.

My mind recollects words here and there
As if the autumnal clouds are roaming after rains
in the air.
Falsely does it travel without the string of work
in the space,
Sometimes it paints in silver, reveals sometimes the
golden colour in grace.
In the corner of the horizon does it build
an image strange,
Again and again it makes in a vacant mind of
lines a change.
That artistry of vapour is as if the neglect of joy,

Nowhere is it responsible, and so it makes the
meaningless game of toy.
Conscious is it to awake and so to be up and
doing in work.
Slumber has nothing to do, and so in distorted dreams
to embark.
The mood of the mind's dream is under the yoke of work,
No holiday does it enjoy in autonomy's park,
With imaginations that crowd in its being free,
Like a flying bird does it build a nest in dream's artistry.
And so feel I the evidence within me
The oldest component of the universe is the dream's insanity.
The process of creation checks it and perennial does it make,
With terrible strength does its authority intake,
The skill of art is to arrest this boisterous fly
For the unreachable to have a try.

☆☆☆

(27)

Vakyer je chhandojal sikhechhi ganthite
Sei jale dhara pare
Adhara ja chetanar satarkata chhila eraiya
Agochare maner gahane.
Name vandhivare chai, na mane namer parichay.
Mulya tar thake yadi
Dine dine hay taha jana
Hate hate phire.
Akasmat parichaye vismay tahar
Bhulay yadi va,
Lokalaye nahi pay sthan
Maner saikattate vikirna se rahe kichhukal,
Lalita ja gopaner
Prakasyer apamane
Dine dine misay valute.
Panyahate achinhita parityekta rikta e jirnata
Juge juge kichhu kichhu diye gechhe akhyater dan
Sahityer bhashamahadwipe
Pranhin pravaler mato.

The web of rhythm of words that I have learnt to weave
Is trapped there
In the unreachable that averts the eyes of alertness
In the depth of mind unseen.
I want to thwart her in name, but name she does deny.
If any worth she has,
Day by day that worth is revealed,
Passes from hand to hand.
If with sudden recognition her surprise
Does entice,
No room she gets in human habitation
For some time in the shores of the mind she does remain
enkindled

Nursed in confidence
In the disgrace of exposure
In sands does unite day by day
This weariness is deserted and empty in the world of hurry,
The gift of the unknown has left something from age to age
In this great island of the language of literature
Like lifeless coral.

☆☆☆

(28)

Miler chumki ganthi chhander parer majhe majhe
Akejo alas vela bhare othe selaiyer kaje.
Arthabhara kichhui-na chokhe kare othe jhilmil
Chharatar phanke phanke mil.
Gachhe gachhe jonakir dal
Kare jhalmal:
Se nahe diper sikha, ratri khela kare andharete
Tukro alok genthe genthe.
Metho gachhe chhoto chhoto phulguli jage,
Vagan hay na tahe ranger phutki ghase lage.
Mane thake kaje lage srishtite se achhe sata sata
Mane thakvar nay seo chharachhari jay kata.
Jharnay jal jhare urvara karite chale mati,
Phenagulo phute othe parakshane jay phati phati.
Kajer sangei khela gantha —
Bhar tahe laghu ray khusi han srishtir vidhata.

Sewing the sparklers amid the veil of rhythm
The workless idle time is in the work of needle fight filled.
The meaningless nothing in eyes dazzles
The rhyme enjoys harmony in blanks
The swarm of crickets on trees
Dazzle;
That is not the flame of the lamp, in darkness the night plays,
Sewing beads of light.
The little flowers in the trees of the meadows awake
That does not a garden create, dots of colour adorn the grass.
It arrests the mind useful as well in hundreds it spreads in the world
Not, of course, to be recalled: it, too, does spread in legion

The water of the spring runs to make the soil fertile
The foams puff up and shatter just afterwards
Work and play are intertwined
The burden is eased for that, and the Lord of creation is
pleased.

☆☆☆

(29)

E jeevane sundarer peyechhi madhur asirvad,
Manusher preetipatre pai tari sudhar aswad.
Duhsaha duhkher dine
Akshata aparajita atmare layechhi ami chine.
Asanna mrityur chhaya jedin karechhi anubhav
Sedin bhayer hate hay ni durval parabhav.
Mahattama manusher sparsa hate hai ni vanchita,
Tander amritavani antarete karechhi sanchita.
Jeevaner vidhatar je dakshinya peyechhi jeevane
Tahari smaranlipi rakhilam sakritajnamane.

The sweet blessings of beauty have I received in this life,
In the urn of human love do I have the taste of drinking pipe.
In unbearable sorrowful days
Known have I the self that unhurt and unbeaten stays.
The day when I have felt the shadow of death in sight,
I faced not defeat meek at the hands of fright.
Ne'er was I from the touch of the greatest men debarred,
Their message of nectar in the heart I have treasured.
The favour of the God of life that I've received in the life
of mine
With grateful mind that memorandum do I entwine.

☆ ☆ ☆

(30)

Dhire sandhya ase, eke eke granthi jata jay skhali
Praharer karmajal hate. Din dila jalanjali
Khuli paschimer singhadwar
Sonar aiswarya tar
Andhakar-aloker sagarsangame.
Dur prabhater pane nata haye nihsavda praname.
Chakshu tar mude ase, esechhe samay
Gabhir dhyaner tale apanar vahya parichay
Karite magan.
Nakshatrer santikshetra asim gagan
Jetha dheke rekhe dey dinasrir arup sattare
Sethay karite labh satya apanare
Kheya dey ratri paravare.

Slowly comes the evening, all the strings loosen
one by one
From the web of hours. The day did sacrifice
Opening the lion-marked western gate
All its golden grandeur
In the marriage of darkness and light
Salutes in silence bending towards the distant east
Slowly closes its eyes down, the time has come
The apparent identity in meditation deep
To be delved.
Where the infinite sky the sphere of blessings of the stars
Covers up the formless existence of the beauty of the day
Truth to be attained there itself
Oars on in the sea of night.

☆ ☆ ☆

(31)

Kshane kshane mane hay javar samay vujhi ela
Vidaydiner' pare avaran phelo
Apragalva suryasta-abhar,
Samay javar
Santa hok stavdha hok, smaransabhar samaroha
Na rachuk soker sammoha.
Vanasreni prasthaner dware
Dharanir santimantra dik mouna pallavsambhare.
Namiya asuk dhire ratrir nihsavda asirvad
Saptarshir jyotir prasad.

Oft do I think as if the time for adieu has come
Cast the veil on the day of farewell
Of the light of the controlled setting sun
Let the parting time
Be peaceful and silent, let not the assembly of condolence
Create the illusion of bereavement.
Let the rows of forest of the door of departure
Proclaim the message of peace of the world with the
assembly of leaves.

Let the silent blessings of the night —
The offerings of the halo of seven saints —
Come down.

(32)

Aloker antare je anander parasan pai
Jani ami tar sathe amar atmar bhed nai.
Ek adi jyotiutsa hate
Chaitanyer punya srote
Amar hayechhe abhisek
Lalate diyechhe jayalekh,
Janayechhe amriter ami adhikari
Param amir sathe jukta hate pari
Vichitra jagate
Praves labhite pari anander pathe.

The touch of joy that in the heart of light I receive
Know I that my soul no difference does conceive.
From an ancient lustrous source
In the holy current of conscious course
Initiated have I been
On the forehead, the mark of victory was given,
It has informed that the source of nectar I know
With the Great I can unite and glow
In this world of wonder
In the avenue of joy I may enter.

☆☆☆

(33)

E amir avaran sahaje skhalita haye jak,
Chaitanyer subhra jyoti
Bhed kari kuhelika
Satyer amrita rup karuk prakas.
Sarva manusher majhe
Ek chiramanaver anandakiran
Chitte mor hok vikeerita.
Sangsarer kshuvdhatar stavdha urdhaloke
Nityer je santirup tai jena dekhe jete pari,
Jeevaner jatil ja vahu nirarthak,
Mithyar vahan jaha samajer kritrim mulyei,
Tai niye kangaler asanta janata
Dure thele diye
E janmer satya artha spashta chokhe jene jai jena
Sima tar perovar age.

Let the cocoon of this self unmask
The bright halo of consciousness
Express the eternal form of Truth
By piercing the mist.
Let the light of joy of a Man Eternal
Amid all men
Be enkindled in my mind.
Beyond the silent world of worldly grievance
Let me behold the blessed form of the Eternal.
Whatever is amply meaningless and critical in this life
Whatever embodies falsehood in the sham value of the society,
Leaving aside all beggarly and
Troubled crowd
Let me know the true meaning with my vivid eyes
Prior to crossing the bar.

☆☆☆

(34)

Aar rekho na andhare amay dekhte dao.
Tomar majhe amar apanare amay dekhte dao.
Kandao jadi kandao ebar, sukher glani soy na je aar,
Jaak-na dhuye nayan amar asrudhare –
Amay dekhte dao.

Jani na to kon kalo ei chhaya
Apon bale bhulay jakhan ghanay bisham maya.
Swapnabhure jamlo bojha, chirajeevan sunyo khoja –
Je mor alo lukiye achhe rater pare
Amay dekhte dao.

Keep me no more in darkness let me behold
Amidst you myself let me behold
If you want to make me weep make so now
No more is the boredom of happiness endeared
Let the eyes with streams of tears be washed away –
Let me behold.
Know I not what blackness this shadow holds
When endeared as own an utter illusion encompasses.
With accumulated burden of dreams futile it is
to seek all thro' life –
My light is hidden beyond the night
Let me behold.

☆☆☆

(35)

Amar andhar bhalo, alor kachhe bikiye debe apnake se.
Alore je lop kare khay sei kuasha sarvaneshe.
Abujh sishu mayer ghare sahaj mone vihar kare,
Abhimani jnani tomar vahir dware theke ese.
Tomar path apanay apni dekhay, tai beye ma, chalbo soja,
Jara path dekhabar bhir kare go tara kebal baray khonja —
Ora oder samarohe bhuliye aane ese dekhi deul paane —
Apan moner vikartake sajiye rakhe devta-veshe.

Good is my darkness, to light it would sell itself out
Disastrous is the mist that wipes off light and eats up.
In the mother's hearth the innocent child roams in an easy mind
The wounded wise in you awaits in the outward door
Your path shows you within, on that path shall I, O mother,
tread straight.
Those who crowd for showing the way simply lengthens the
period of search
They implicate me in their arrangements, towards the
courtyard do I come and see
In the guise of gods do they decorate the perversions of
their own minds.

☆☆☆

(36)

Asim kalsagare bhuvan bhese chalechhe.
Amritabhavan kotha achhe taha ke jane.
Hero apan hridaymajhe dubiye, e ki shobha!
    Amritamoy devata satata
Viraje ei mandire, ei sudhaniketane.

The world goes afloating in the endless sea of time
Who knows where the abode of nectar lies
Behold dipping in the midst of your heart,
                    what a scene this is!
The god full of nectar
Always heralds in this temple, this abode of juice.

☆☆☆

(37)

Ekhono andhar rayechhe he nath –
E pran deen malin, chit adhir,
Sab sunyamoy.
Chari dike chahi, path nahi nahi –
Shanti kotha, kotha aaloy?
Kotha taapahari pipasar bari –
Hridayer chira-asray.

Darkness still persists, O Lord –
Poor and dirty this life is, restless is the mind.
Everything full of emptiness.
I look around, no, no way is there
Where is peace, where the abode?
Where is water to ward off heat to quench the thirst –
The eternal resort of the heart?

☆☆☆

(38)

Dekha jadi dile chhero na aar, ami ati dinahin.
Nahi ki hetha paap moha vipadrashi.
Toma bina ekela nahi bharasa.

Leave no more when thou hast shown thy appearance
Greatly poor and distressed am I
Are there no sin, enchantment and an array of dangers here?
Bereft of thee, no hope for me in being alone.

☆☆☆

(39)

Din to chali gelo Prabhu, britha – katare kande hiya
Jeevan aharaha hatechhe ksheen – kee halo e sunyo jeevane.
Dekhabo kemane ei mlan mukh, kachhe jabo kee laiya
Prabhu he, jaibe bhay, pavo bharasa
Tumi jadi dako e adhame.

In vain, O Lord, did the day wane – the heart weeps in sorrow.
Life is shortening every now and then –
What did I fare in this empty life,
How would I this ematiated countenance show,
With what should I approach Him?
O Lord, no fear would be there, with hope would I be beamed
If thou callest on this hopeless one.

☆☆☆

(40)

Dubi amritapathare — jai bhule charachar,
Milay rabi sashi,
Nahi desh, nahi kaal, nahi heri seema —
Premamurati hridaye jage,
Ananda nahi dhare.

In the sea of nectar do I immerse — the world do I forget
The sun and the moon are in unison.
No country, no time, no end do I behold
The image of love does awaken in the heart.
Joy o'erfloods.

☆☆☆

(41)

Peyechhi abhaypad, aar bhay kare —
Anande chalechhi bhabaparabarpare.
Madhur sheetal chhay shok taap dure jaay.
Karunakiran tar arun vikashe.
Jeevanemarane aar kabhu na chharibo tare.

Blessed am I with the feet of the Fearless,
whom do I fear any more?
Towards the shore of the sea of the world
Am I plying on in pleasure
Pleasant and cool is the shadow
Bereavement and emotion leave apart
The sun shines His light of pity
Never shall I leave Him in life and death any more.

☆☆☆

(42)

Haay ke dibe aar santwana.
Sakale giyechhe he, tumi jeyo na –
Chaho prasanna nayane Prabhu, din adhin jane
Chari dike chai, heri na kahare.
Keno gele phele ekela andhare –
Hero he sunyo bhuvan mamo.

Alas, who else would console me
Everything is gone, O depart not –
With pleasing eyes behold, O Lord, this poor and submitted person
I look around and behold none
Why did you desert me in lonely darkness –
O behold my empty world.

☆☆☆

(43)

Amareo karo marjana.
Amareo deho Nath amriter kana
Griha chhere pathe ese base achhi mlan beshe
Amaro hridaye karo ason rachana.
Jani ami, ami tuba malin santan –
Amareo dite habe padatale sthan.
Apani dubechhi pape, kanditechhi manastape –
Shuno go amaro ei manovedana.

Pardon me, too.
Give me, too, O Lord, the particle of nectar,
Leaving home, seated am I on the way
Have thy seat on my heart as well.
Know I, a dirty son of thine am I –
At thy feet I, too, shall be given a room.
Myself in sin am I drowned, in mental agony
am I weeping
O listen the pains of my heart as well.

☆☆☆

(44)

Din jaay re din jaay bisade –
Swarthakolahale, chhalanay, bifala basanay.
Esechhe kshanatare, kshanapare jaaibe chale,
Janam kaate brithay badbibade kumantranay.

Days pass on sorrowful days do wane –
In ukase of the self, in strategies fruitless hopes
For a moment hast thou come, wouldst bid farewell
after a moment

In vain does life pass in quarrels and vile policies.

(45)

Prabhu, khelechhi anek khela — ebe tomar kror chahi
Sranta hridaye he, tomari prasad chahi.
Aji chintatapta prane taba santibari chahi.
Aji sarbabitto chhari tomay nityanitya chahi.

Lord, many a play have I played — now your lap
do I want.
O in tired heart your offerings do I want.
With life baked in thoughts today, your sprinkling of blessings
do I want
Leaving all wealth today, all the time ye do I want.

☆ ☆ ☆

(46)

Vani taba dhay ananta gagane loke loke,
Taba vani graha chandra dipto tapan tara.
Sukh dukh taba vani, janam maran vani tomar,
Nibhrito gabhir taba vani bhakta hridaye santidhara.

The message rushes on towards the boundless sky from
one hemisphere to the other
Thy message is like a planet or the moon, or the
shining sun or stars
Happiness and sorrow encompass thy message,
birth and death thy message too.
The message of thine, lonely and sombre, is like a spring
of peace in the heart of the devotee.

☆ ☆ ☆

(47)

Kemane rakhibi tora tare lukaye
Chandrama tapan tara apan alokchhaye.
He vipul sansar, sukhe duhkhe andhar,
Katakal rakhibi dhaki tahare kuhelikay!
Atma-vihari tini, hridaye uday tar –
Naba naba mahima jaage, naba naba kiran bhaay.

How would ye keep Him hidden
In the own shadow under the moon, the sun
or the stars?
O the family vast and dark in happiness and
sorrow
How long would ye cover Him in the mirage?
A soul-traveller He is, His awakening is in the
heart
A newer grandeur adorns, a new aura of light
flashes.

☆☆☆

(48)

Bhuvan haite bhuvanbasi eso apan hridaye.
Hridaymajhe hridaynath achhe nitya sath sath –
Kotha phirichho divarat, hero tahare abhaye.
Hetha chira anandadham, hetha vajichhe abhay naam,
Hetha puribe sakal kaam nibhrita amrita-alaye.

Come to your own heart. O resident of the world
The Lord of the heart is amid the heart all the time
Where are you roaming day and night, behold Him fearlessly.
The eternal abode of joy is here, the fearless name is
ringing at this place.
All desires would be fulfilled here in the nectar-abode of
silence.

☆☆☆

(49)

Ichchha jabe habe laiyo paare,
Pujakusume rachiya anjali
Achhi base bhabasindhu-kinare.
Jata din rakho toma mukh chahi
Phullamane rabo e songsare.
Dakibe jakhani tomar sebake
Druta chali jaibo chhari sabare.

Take me to the heaven whenever you wish
Preparing offerings with flowers of worship
On the edge of the sea of the world am I seated.
Looking at your countenance
With a pleasant mind shall I remain as you
please in this world.
Whenever you call on your servant,
Leaving all shall I quickly depart.

☆☆☆

(50)

Premanande rakho purno amare divasraat.
Viswabhuvane nirakhi satata sundar tomare,
Chandra-Surya-kirane tomar karun nayanapaat.
Sukhasampade kari he paan taba prasadbaari.
Dukhasankate paras paai taba mangalahaat.
Jeevane jwalo amar deep taba ananta aasha,
Maran-ante hauk tomari charane suprabhat.
Laho laho mamo sab ananda, sakal preeti-geeti —
Hridaye bahire ekmatro tumi amar nath.

With joy of love thou dost keep me filled in day and night
All the time do I behold thee beautiful in the universe.
Thy eyelids are piteous with the light of the moon and the sun.
Thy water of gifts do I drink in happiness and affluence.
In sorrows and dangers do I feel the touch of thy auspicious hands.
Enkindle thy eternal lamp in the life with boundless hopes
Let good morning usher forth at the end of death on thy feet.
Take, take all my joys, all love and songs —
Beyond my heart thou art my lone lord.

☆☆☆

(51)

Chira-purano chand,
Chiradibas emni theko, amar ei saadh.
Purano hasi purano sudha mitay mamo purano kshudha –
Nutan kono chakor jeno paay na parasad.

The ever old moon,
Remain so all day ever, this is my desire
The old laughter the old juice quench my old thirst
Let no new aspiring bird be blessed with the offering.

☆☆☆

(52)

Kata kal rabe balo Bharat re
Sudhu dal bhaat jal pathya kare.
Deshe annajaler halo ghor anatan –
Dharo whisky-soda aar murgi-mutton.
Jaao thakur chaitan-chutki niya –
Eso dari nari Kalimaddi Mian.

How long shall ye remain, O India,
Only with pulses, rice and water as thy diet?
A grave scarcity of food and drink is in the country
Take recourse to whisky-soda and chicken or mutton
Depart, O priest, with the pigtail
Come, Kalimaddi Mian, let's move the beard!

☆☆☆

(53)

Swarge tomay niye jabe uriye –
Pichhe pichhe ami chalbo khunriye,
Ichchha habe tikir daga dhare
Vishnuduter mathata dei gunriye.

To the heaven will ye be taken aflying
Limping on shall I follow
Catching hold of the end of the pigtail
I wish to crush the head of the messenger
of Vishnu.

☆☆☆

(54)

Ami kebal phool jogabo
Tomar duti ranga haate
Buddhi amar khele naako
Pahara ba mantranate.

Only flowers do I supply
At thy two shining hands
My intellect does not play
With watch or advice.

☆☆☆

(55)

Ogo hridaybaner shikari
Michhe tare jule dhara je tomari bhikhari.
Sahasrabar payer kaachhe apni je jan mare aachhe
Nayanvaner khoncha khete se je anadhikari.

O the hunter of the forest of the heart
Vain it is to entrap Him who pines for you.
One who remains dead a thousand times at the feet
Fails to receive the pricks of the arrows of eyes.

☆☆☆

(56)

Kaar hate je dhara debo haay
Tai bhabte amar bela jaay.
Daan dikete takai jakhan bayer lagi kande re mon —
Bayer dike phirle takhan dakhin daake 'aay re aay'.

Alas, to whom shall I surrender
Thinking so, my day wanes.
When do I look to the right the mind weeps for the left
And as I then turn to the left, the right beckons 'come, ye come'.

☆☆☆

(57)

Virahe maribo bale chhilo mone pon,
Ke tora vahute bandhi karili baaron.
Bhebechhinu asrujale dubibe akultale —
Kahar sonar tari karilo taaron.

In languishment would I die and that was
my promise
Who are ye that forbade me by holding in
your hands?
I thought with tears would I drown myself
in the endless depth.
Whose golden boat did drift me away?

☆☆☆

(58)

He sakha, mamo hridaye raho.
Sangsare sab kaje dhyane jnane hridaye raho.
Nath, tumi eso dhire, sukh-dukh-hasi-nayannire,
Laho amar jeevan ghire –
Sangsare sab kaje dhyane jnane hridaye raho.

O Friend, remain in my heart.
Remain in the world in all work and meditation,
in knowledge, in the heart.
Lord, come ye slowly in happiness or sorrow,
in laughter or in tears.
Hold me encompassing my life –
Remain in the world in all work and meditation,
in knowledge, in the heart.

☆☆☆

(59)

Dako more aji e nishithe
Nidramagan jabe visvajagat,
Hridaye asiye nirabe dako he
    Tomari amrite.
Jwalo taba deep e antaratimire,
Bar bar dako mamo acheta chite.

Call on me tonight at dead hours
When the whole universe is wrapt in sleep
O call on me, coming silently in my heart
    With thy nectar.
Enkindle thy lamp in the darkness of this mind,
Beckon time and again my unconscious mind.

☆☆☆

(60)

Ami kee bale karibo nivedan
Amar hriday pran mon.
Chitte asi daya kari nije laho apahari,
Karo tare apanari dhan – amar hriday pran mon.
Sudhu dhuli, sudhu chhai, mulya jar kichhu nai,
Mulya tare karo samarpan sparshe taba parashratan!
Tomari gourabe jabe amar gourab habe
Sab tabe dibo visarjan –
Amar hriday pran mon.

With what utterance shall I submit
My heart, life and mind!
Do please come to the mind and accept thyself stealthily,
Thy own wealth do thou make it – my heart, life and mind.
Only dust or ash whate'er of no worth
Be worthy with thy magical touch.
When thy glory will be mine
Everything would I then sacrifice –
My heart, life and mind.

☆☆☆

(61)

Bajao tumi kabi, tomar sangeet sumadhur
Gambhiratar tane prane mamo –
Draba jeevan jharibe jhara jhara nirjhar taba paaye.
Bisaribo sab sukh-dukh, chinta, atripta basana –
Bicharibe vimukta hriday vipul viswa-majhe
Anukhan ananda baye.

Play on, O poet, your pleasant music
With more serene tune in my life –
Like a fountain, the soluble life will sprinkle
at your feet.
All happiness and sorrow, thoughts and insatiated
desires shall I sacrifice.
The emancipated heart would ever wander in the
wide world
Amidst the joyous wind.

☆☆☆

(62)

E Bharate rakho nitya Prabhu tabo subho asirvad –
Tomar abhay, tomar ajita amrita vani,
Tomar sthir amar asha.
Anirvan dharma alo sabar urdhe jwalo jwalo,
Sankate durdine he
Rakho ture aranye tomari pathe.
Vakshe bandhi dao tar varma taba nirvidar,
Nihsanke jena sanchare nirbheek.
Paaper nirakhi joy nishtha tabuo roy –
Thake taba charane atal viswase.

Lord, ever confer thy auspicious blessings upon this India –
Thy fearless, thy unvanquished nectarlike message,
Thy firm deathless expectations.
Enkindle, O kindle light, the unextinguished religion, above all
In crisis and rainy days,
Place it along the forest on thy path.
Encompass his breast with thy unpiercing armour.
So that he might traverse *sans* fear.
Beholding the victory of vice, sincerity still persists –
With firm faith does adorn thy feet.

☆☆☆

(63)

Swapan jadi bhangile rajaniprabhate
Purno karo hiya mangalakirane
Rakho more taba kaje,
Nabin karo e jeevan he.
Khuli mor grihadwar dako tomari bhavane he.

If thou dost shatter the dream at the dawn of night
With auspicious light fill in my heart.
Keep me in thy service
O make this life young.
Opening the door of my room, O call on me at
thy mansion.

☆☆☆

(64)

Manomohan, gahan jaminiseshe
Dile amare jagaye.
Meli dile shubho prate supto e ankhi
Shubhro alok lagaye.
Mithya swapanraji kotha milaila,
Andhar gelo milaye.
Santisarasi majhe chittakamal
Phutilo anandabaye.

O enchanter of mind, at the end of dense night
Thou didst awaken me.
In the auspicious morn, thou didst unfold these eyes asleep
With the touch of white light.
Where did the vain array of dreams disappear!
Darkness was merged.
Amid the stream of peace, the lotus of the mind
Bloomed in the joyous wind.

☆☆☆

(65)

Amare karo jeevandan,
Preran karo antare taba ahaban.
Asichhe kato jaay kato, pai sata harai sata —
Tomari paye rakho achal mor pran.
Dao more mangalbrata, swartha karo dure prahata —
Thamaye vifal sandhan jagao chitte satya jnan.
Labhe kshatite sukhe-soke andhakare diba-aloke
Nirbhaye vahi nischal mane taba vidhan.

Bless me with the gift of life.
Send thy beckoning in the heart.
Much comes and much goes, much do I receive and much lose —
Keep my life steady at thy feet.
Give me the auspicious devotion, strike off all interest of the self
Resisting all baffled search, awaken truth and knowledge
in the mind.
In gain and loss, happiness and bereavement, in darkness
and daylight
Thy ordains do I fearlessly carry out in the unmoved mind.

☆☆☆

(66)

Je tore pagal bale tare tui balish ne kichhu.
Ajke tore kemon bhebe ange je tor dhulo debe
Kal se prate mala hate asbe re tor pichhu pichhu.
Ajke apon maner bhare thak se base gadir 'pare –
Kalke preme asbe neme, karbe se tar matha nichu.

Say nothing to him who calls you insane
One who, thinking you otherwise, throws dust today o'er
the limbs
With a garland would he come tomorrow and follow you.
Let him remain seated on the seat with a puffed up
mind of his own today
With love would he descend tomorrow, and would bend
down his head.

☆☆☆

(67)

Naba naba pallavaraji
Sab ban upabane uthe vikashiya
Dakinpavane sangeet uthe baji.
Madhur sugandhe akul bhuban, haha karichhe mamo jeevan.
Eso eso sadhanar dhan, mamo mon purno karo aji.

The new clusters of leaves
Spring forth in all forests and groves,
Music plays in the southern wind.
With sweet fragrance the world is flooded, desolate is my
heart in emptiness
Come, O come, the gift of meditation, fill in my mind today.

☆☆☆

(68)

Veena bajao he mamo antare.
Sajane bijane, bandhu, sukhe duhkhe vipade –
Anandita taan shunao he mamo antare.

O play on the *veena* in my heart.
In companion or in solitude, O friend, in happiness,
sorrow or adversity
Make me listen to the pleasant tune in my heart.

☆☆☆

(69)

Mamo angane swami anande hase.
Sugandha bhase ananda-raate.
    Khule dao duar sab,
    Sabare dako dako,
Nahi rekho kothao kono badha –
Oho, aji sangeete mon pran maate.

In joy my Lord laughs in my courtyard
Sweet smell permeates the joyous night.
    Open all the doors
    Call, call everyone.
Allow no constraint anywhere
Aha, in songs is my mind enamoured today!

☆☆☆

(70)

Timirduar kholo — eso, eso neerav charane.
Janani amar, danrao ei naveen arunkirane.
Punyaparashpulake sab aalas jak dure.
Gagane vajuk veena jagat-jagano sure.
Janani, jeevan jurao taba prasad sudha sameerane
Janani amar, danrao mamo jyotibibhasito nayane.

Open the door of darkness — come, come in silent footsteps.
My mother, stand in this young sunlight.
With the joy of virtuous touch, let all indolence be away.
Let the *veena* play on in the sky in the world-awakening tune.
Mother, embalm life with the air of the juice of thy offerings.
Mother mine, stand before my eyes hallowed with lustre.

☆☆☆

(71)

More bare bare phirale.
Pujaphool na phutilo dukhanisha na chhutilo
Na tutilo avaran.
Jeevan bhari madhuri kee shubholagane jagibe?
Nath, ohe Nath, kabe labe tanu mon dhan?

Time and again did you turn me away.
The flowers for worship did not bloom, the night
of sorrow did not pass
Nor was the veil cut off.
On what auspicious moment will efflorescene
shine forth all thro' life?
Lord, O Lord, when would you accept my body, mind
and wealth?

☆☆☆

(72)

Aji nahi nahi nidra ankhipate
Tomar bhavantale heri pradip jwale,
Dure bahire timire ami jagi jorhate.
    Krandan dhwanichhe pathhara pabane,
    Rajani murchhagata vidyutghate.
    Dwar kholo he dwar kholo –
Prabhu, koro daya, deho dekha dukhorate.

No, no slumber is there in eyelids today
At thy residence do I behold the trimming lamp –
With folded hands do I remain awake in darkness
outside from a distance
In the waylost wind the wailing is going on
The night is fainted with the stroke of lightning.
Open the door, O open the door
Lord, be kind, show thyself in the sorrowful night.

☆☆☆

(73)

Amra basbo tomar sane —
Tomar sharik habo rajar raja,
Tomar adhek sinhasane.
Tomar dwari moder karechhe, shir nata —
Tara janena je moder garab kata.
Tai vahir hate tomay daki,
Tumi deke lao go apon jane.

We would sit beside thee,
O King of kings, we would be thy partners
to thy seat as a half.
Thy door-keepers have hung down our heads
They know not how proud we are.
So we call on thee from outside.
O call on and accept thy endearing persons.

☆☆☆

(74)

Tumi kichhu diye jao mor prane gopane go –
Phuler gandha vanshir gaane, marmarmukharita pavane
Tumi kichhu niye jao vedana hate vedane –
Je mor asru hasite leen, je vani neerav nayane.

O give something stealthily in my life –
In the fragrance of flowers in the songs of the flute,
in the murmuring wind
Take ye something from pains to pains –
The tears of mine mingled in smile,
The message in silent eyes.

☆☆☆

(75)

Amriter sagare ami jabo jabo re,
Trishna jwalichhe mor prane.
Kotha path balo he balo, byethar byethi he –
Kotha hate kaladhwani asichhe kane.

In the sea of nectar shall I go, O I shall go
Thirst in my life is burning.
Where's the way, O tell me tell, O partner of my pain
Wherefrom is the murmuring sound coming.

☆☆☆

(76)

Joy taba vichitra ananda he kavi,
Joy tomar karuna
Joy taba bhisan sab-kalush-nashan rudrata.
Joy amrita taba, joy mrityu taba,
Joy shok taba, joy santwana.
Joy purnajagrata jyoti taba
Joy timirnibir nishithini bhaydayini.
Joy premmadhumoy milan taba joy asaha vichchhed vedana.

Victory, O poet, to thy diverse joy,
Victory to thy pity.
Victory to thy terrible fury of eliminating all darkness
Victory to thy nectar, victory to thy death
Victory to thy bereavement, victory to
thy consolation
Victory to thy full awakening lustre
Victory to dense dark night fearful
Victory to thy union full of pleasant love
Victory to unbearable pain of separation.

☆☆☆

(77)

Kar milan chao virahi –
Tahare kotha khunjichho bhaba-aranye –
Kutil jatil gahane santihin ore mon.
Dekho dekho re chittakamale charanpadma raje – hay!
Amritajyoti kiba sundar ore mon.

Whose unison do you want, O exponent of languishment
Where are you seeking Him in the forest of the world
O mind *sans* peace, in the vicious complex poignance.
Behold, O behold the lotuslike feet adorn in the
lotus of the mind, ah!
O mind, how marvellous is the nectarlike lustre!

☆☆☆

(78)

Jadi jharer megher mato ami dhai chanchal-antar
Tabe daya karo he, daya karo he, daya karo Iswar.
Ohe apappurush, dinahin ami esechhi paper kule –
Prabhu daya karo he, daya karo he, daya kare lao tule.
Ami jaler majhare baas kari, tabu trisay sukaye mari –
Prabhu daya karo he, daya kare dao hriday sudhay bhari.

If like the cloud of a storm do I rush on with a restless mind,
O God, be kind, be kind, be kind to me.
O the person *sans* sin, on the shore of vice have I arrived
poor and deserted
O Lord, be kind, be kind, be kind and take me up.
Amidst water do I live yet I pine for thirst and die
O Lord, be kind, be kind in filling my heart in pleasantness.

☆☆☆

(79)

Puspa phute kon kunjabane,
Kon nibhrite re, kon gahane.
Matila akul dakshinvayu souravchanchal sancharane.
Katila klanta vasanta nisha vahir-angan-sangisane,
Utsavraj viraja kotha ke layi jabe se bhavane.

In which forest of flowers do flowers bloom
O in which solitude and silence!
In restless movement of fragrance the southern
wind intoxicated itself
The tired night of spring passed amid companions in
the outward courtyard
O king of ceremonies, where do ye adorn, who will
escort to that residence?

☆☆☆

(80)

Darao mon, ananta brahmanda-majhe anandasabhabhavane aaj.
Vipul mahimay gagane mahasane viraj kare viswaraj.
Sindhu saila tatini maharanya jaladharmala
Tapan chandra tara gabhir mandre gahichhe suno gaan.
Ei visva mahotsav dekhi magan hala sukhe kavi chitta,
Bhuli gela sav kaaj.

Stand, O mind, amidst endless universe in the mansion of
the joyous meeting today
In unending grandeur the lord of the universe adorns
the great seat in the firmament
The sea and the mountain, the rivers and the great forests
The strings of clouds and the sun, the moon and the stars
Listen to the songs they are singing in poignance.
Beholding this great ceremony of the universe,
The poet's mind was absorbed in happiness
And forgot all activities.

☆☆☆

(81)

Ja hariye jaay ta agle base raibo kata aar?
Aar parine raat jugte he Nath, bhavte anivar.
Aachhi ratri divas dhare duar amar vandha kare,
Aaste je chay sandehe tay tarai vare var,
Tai to karo hoy na asa amar eka ghare.
Anandamoy bhuvan tomar vaire khela kare.
Tumio vujhi path nahi pao, ese ese phiriya jao –
Rakhe ja chai roy na tao, dhulay ekakar.

How long shall I remain seated, guarding one that gets lost?
No more can I remain awake at night O Lord, to
ceaselessly think.
Day and night do I exist closing my doors
Time and again do I drive away one who wants to come,
in doubt.
And so in my lonely room none arrives.
Thy pleasing world plays outside.
Perhaps, ye, too, get no avenue, ye come and go back
Whate'er I want to preserve remains not, everything
merges in the dust.

☆☆☆

(82)

Ei malin bastra chharte habe, habe go eibar –
Amar ei malin ahankar.
Diner kaje dhula laagi anek daage halo daagi,
Emni tapta haye achhe sahya kara bhar
Amar ei malin ahankar.
Ekhon to kaj sanga hala diner avasane –
Hala re tar asar samay, asha elo prane.
Snan kare aay ekhon tabe premer vasan parte habe,
Sandhyabaner kusum tule ganthte habe haar.
Ore aay, samay nei je aar.

This dirty dress will have to be given up, O to be left now—
This dirty pride of mine.
With dust in day's work much stain sprinkles
So heated it is that it is beyond tolerance
This dirty pride of mine.
In day's end all work came to an end
Now is the time for His arrival, hope springs forth
in the heart
Come now after a bath, the clothings of love will have
to be put on.
Plucking the flowers of the forest of evening,
garlands will have have to be sewn.
O come, no more time is there.

☆☆☆

(83)

Nibhrita praner devata jekhane jagen eka,
Bhakta, sethay kholo dwar — aaj labo tar dekha.
Saradin sudhu vahire ghure ghure kare chahi re
    Sandhyavelar arati hoyni amar sekha.
    Tava jeevaner alote jeevanpradip jwali
    He pujari, aaj nibhrite sajabo amar thali.
Jetha nikhiler sadhana pujalok kare rachana
    Sethay amio dharibo ekti jyotir rekha.

Where the God of silent heart awakes alone,
O devotee, open the door there, I'd visit Him today
Wandering all day alone outside, whom do I want
    I'm yet to learn the evening *arati.*
    Trimming the lamp of life with the light of thy life
    O worshipper, in silence shall I arrange my offerings today
Where the meditation of the universe creates the world of devotion.
I, too, would follow the line of a halo there.

☆☆☆

(84)

Jarjar prane Nath, barisan karo taba premsudha –
Nibaro e hridaydahan.
Karo he mochan karo sab papmoha,
Dur karo bishoybasana.

In the distressed heart O Lord shower thy stream of love
Extinguish this fire of the heart.
Drive O drive all sins and enchantments away
Drive off all yearnings of things.

☆☆☆

(85)

Rakho rakho re jeevane jeevana ballava
Pranamane dhari rakho nivire anandavandhane.
Alo jwalo hridayadeepe atinibhrita antaramajhe,
Akuliya dao pran gandhachandane.

Keep, O keep the friend of life in the life
Hold him heart and soul in close strings of joy
Enkindle the lamp of the heart amid the very secret mind
With fragrant sandal overflood life.

☆☆☆

(86)

Timirmoy nibir nisha nahi re nahi disha –
Ekela ghanaghor pathe, pantha, kotha jao.
Bipath dukh nahi jano, badha kichhu nahi mano,
Andhakar hatechha paar — kahar sara pao.
Deep hridaye jwale, nibe na se bayu bale –
Mahanande nirantar e kee gaan gao.
Sammukhe abhay taba, pashchate abhayrav –
Antare bahire kahar mukh chao.

Full of darkness is the dense night : no, O no direction is there
Alone in the deep dense path, where, O traveller, do you go?
Know ye neither the sufferings of wrong path nor do ye care
any constraint
Darkness are ye crossing — whose response do ye receive.
The lamp burns in the heart, it extinguishes not, the
wind says –
What song do ye continually sing in great joy.
Fearlessness is ahead of thee the sound of fearlessness
is behind
Whose countenance do ye behold in the mind and outside?

☆☆☆

(87)

Visva jakhan nidramagan, gagan andhakar,
Ke dey amar veenar tare emon jhankar.
Nayane ghoom nilo kere, uthe vasi shayan chhere –
Mele ankhi cheye thaki, pai ne dekha tar.
Gunjariya gunjariya pran uthila pure,
Jani ne kon vipul vani vaje vyekul sure.
Kon vedanay vujhina re hriday bhara asrubhare,
Pariye dite chai kahare apon kanthahar.

When the world is rapt in slumber and the sky is dark
Who is He giving such a jolt in the strings of my *veena*?
Sleep bade farewell to eyes, leaving bed I remain seated
Opening eyes I stare, I fail to meet Him.
The heart was full with the humming tune
Know not I what enormous message plays on in restless tunes.
O I fail to understand in what a pain with
heartful burden of tears.
Whom I want to adorn with my own necklace.

☆☆☆

(88)

Ebar nirav kare dao he tomar mukhar kavire,
Tar hriday vanshi apni kere vajao gabhire.
Nisithrater nivir sure vanshite tan dao he pure,
Je tan diye abak karo grahashashire.
Ja-kichhu mor chhariye achhe jeevan-marane
Gaaner tane miluk ese tomar charane.
Vahudiner vakyarasi ek nimeshe jave bhasi —
Ekla vase shunbo vanshi akul timire.

O make your tumultuous poet silent now
Seize his flute of the heart and play on in poignance.
With intense tune of midnight O fill in notes in the flute,
With which you startle the planets and the moon.
Whate'er is spread in my life and death
Be in unison at your feet with the beckoning of songs.
The volleys of sentences of many days would in a moment
float away —
Sitting alone I would listen to the flute in shoreless darkness.

☆☆☆

(89)

Jatabar alo jwalate chai, nibe jay bare bare.
Amar jeevane tomar asan gabhir andhakare.
Je latati achhe shukayechhe mool — kunri dhare shudhu,
nahi phote phool.
Amar jeevane taba seva tai vedanar upahare.
Poojagourav punyabibhav kichhu nahi, nahi lesh —
E taba poojari pariya esechhe lajjar deen vesh.
Utsave tar ase nai keha, vaje nai vanshi, saje nai geha,
Kandiya tomay enechhe dakiya bhangamandir-dware.

Everytime I want to put on the light, it extinguishes
In my life your seat lies in deep darkness.
The creeper that exists is with its dried root — only buds are
there and no flower blooms.
So your service in my life is in the gift of pains.
The glory of worship or the grandeur of virtue is no more,
not even any trace —
Here is your worshipper with the poor dress of shame on.
Nobody came in his ceremony, no flute played on, rooms *sans*
any decoration
He has called on you a-weeping at the door of the broken
temple.

☆ ☆ ☆

(90)

Vajre tomar vaje vanshi, se ki sahaj gaan,
Sei surete jagbo ami, dao more sei kaan,
Bhulbe na aar sahajete, sei prane mon uthbe mete
Mrityu-majhe dhaka achhe je antahin pran.
Se jhar jeno soi anande chittaveener tare
Saptasindhu dashdiganta nachao je jhankare.
Aram hate chhinna kare sei gabhire lao go more
Ashantir antare jethay shanti sumahan.

In thunder your flute plays on. Is that a simple song?
In that very tune would I awake, give me those ears.
No more would I forget in simplicity, the mind would be intoxicated
with that endless life
Encapsulated in the midst of death.
May I in joy forbear that storm in the strings of
the *veena* of my mind.
With resonance do you make the seven seas and the
ten horizons dance.
Tearing off from comfort O take me to that poignance.
Where peace with all fine grandeur lies in the heart of
disturbance.

☆☆☆

(91)

Daya diye habe go mor jeevan dhute
Naile ki aar parbo tomar charan chhunte.
Tomay dite pujar dali beriye pare sakal kali
Paran amar pari ne tai paye thute.
Eto din to chhila na mor kono vyatha,
Sarva ange makha chhila malinata
Aaz oi subhra koler tare vyakul hriday kende mare –
Diyo na go diyo na aar dhulay shute.

O with kindness will my life have to be cleaned
Or would I be able to touch thy feet any more!
In offering thee the casket of worship all dirt comes out
Which is why I could not place may heart on thy feet.
No pain was there for me so long,
Dirtiness was spread all o'er my body.
Today for that clean lap the pining heart dies a-weeping –
Allow not O no more allow to sleep on the dust.

☆☆☆

(92)

Chitta amar haralo aaz megher majhkhane –
Kothay chhute chalechhe she kothay ke jaane.
Vijuli tar veenar tare aghat kare bare bare,
Vooker majhe vajra vaje kee mahatane.
Punja punja bhare bhare nivir neel andhakare
Jaralo re anga amar, chharalo prane.
Pagal haoa nritye mati halo amar sather sathi –
Atta hase dhay kotha she, varon na mane.

My mind today is lost in the midst of clouds
None knows where it is rushing on.
Lightning strikes again and again in its *veena's* strings
In what a great tune thunder plays on in the breast!
With clustered burdens amid deep blue darkness
My limbs were covered and spread in the life.
The mad wind being intoxicated in the dance
became my companion
Where does it rush on in bursting laughter, it cares not
any restraint.

☆☆☆

(93)

Oi re tari dilo khule.
Tor bojha ke nebe tule.
Samne jakhan jabi ore thak-na pichhan pichhe pare —
Pithe tare baite geli, ekla pare raili kule.
Gharer bojha tene tene parer ghate rakhli ene —
Tai je tore bare bare phirte halo, geli bhule.
Daak re abar majhire daak, bojha tomar jaak bhese jaak—
Jeevankhani ujar kare sape de tar charanmule.

O yonder the boat was unfastened.
Who would carry up your burden?
As you go ahead, why not remain behind?
On the back did you want to carry him, and so on the shore
did you remain alone.
Pulling the burden of the room on the bank did you store
Which is why you had to come back time and again,
and forget
O call on the boatman again, let your burden be
washed away.
Unfolding the life wide open, submit it in front of
his feet.

☆☆☆

(94)

Mahaviswe mahakashe mahakalmajhe
Ami manav kee lagi ekaki bhrami vismaye.
Tumi achho viswanath, asheem rahashyamajhe
Neerave ekaki taba alaye.
Ami chahi toma-pane —
Tumi more niyata herichho, nimeshvihin nata nayane.

In the great universe, in the space amidst the great time
I a man know not why I wander in astonishment.
Amid endless mystery, the Lord of the universe.
In silence thou art alone in thy residence.
Looking towards thee
Do I behold thou art continually seeing me with
ceaseless bent eyes.

☆☆☆

(95)

Aji mamo jeevane namichhe dhire
Ghana rajani neerave nivirgambhire.
Jago aji jago, jagore tare laye —
    Premaghana hridaymandire.

Slowly is plunging the dense night in my life
In silence and in deep poignance.
Awake, awake today, O awake with Him
    In the love-clasped temple of the heart.

☆☆☆

(96)

Pantha ekhono keno alasita anga —
Hero, puspavane jage vihanga.
Gagan magan nandan alok-ullase,
Loke loke uthe prantaranga.
Ruddha hridaykakshe timire
Keno atmasukhdukkhe shayan —
Jago jaga, chalo mangalpathe
Yatridale mili laho viswer sanga.

Traveller, why with idle limbs even now!
Behold, birds awake in the flower garden
The sky is rapt in the laughter of heavenly light
The waves of life surge in people everywhere.
In the closed room of the heart in darkness
Why are you laid in self happiness and sorrow?
Awake, awake, tread on the auspicious path,
Take the companionship of the universe by being
in unison with the group of travellers.

☆☆☆

(97)

Pratidin taba gatha gabo ami sumadhur –
Tumi deho more katha, tumi deho more sur –
Tumi jadi thako mone vikacha kamalasane,
Tumi jadi karo pran taba preme bharpoor.
Tumi shono jadi gaan amar samukhe thaki,
Sudha jadi kare daan tomar udar ankhi,
Tumi jadi dukh-pare rakho kar snehabhare,
Tumi jadi sukh hate dambha karahe door.

Everyday shall I sing thy pleasant song —
Give me speech, give me tunes —
If thou dost remain in the mind in the serene lotus seat
If thou dost fill in life with thy love
If thou dost listen to the song in front of me
If thou with generous eyes shower the juice as a gift
If thou dost place thy affectionate hands upon sorrow
If thou dost drive away pride from happiness.

☆☆☆

(98)

Pratidin ami, he Jeevanswami, danrabo tomari sammukhe.
Kari jorkar, he Bhubaneswar, danrabo tomari sammukhe.
Tomar apar akasher tale bijane birale he –
Namra hridaye nayaner jale danrabo tomari sammukhe.
Tomar vichitra e bhavasangsare karmaparavarpare he –
Nikhil bhuvanloker majhare danrabo tomari sammukhe.
Tomar e bhave mamo karma jabe samapan habe he,
Ogo Rajaraj, ekaki neerave danrabo tomari sammukhe.

O Lord of life, everyday shall I stand before thee.
With folded palms, O Lord of the universe, shall I stand before thee.
Under thy boundless sky, O in silence and loneliness.
With benign heart and tears shall I stand before thee.
O in thy diverse world on the sea-shore of work
Amidst the vast universe shall I stand before thee.
O when I shall complete my work in this world
O King of kings, alone shall I silently stand before thee.

☆☆☆

(99)

Amar e ghare apanar kare grihadeepkhani jwalo.
Sab dukhshok sarthak hok labhiya tomari alo.
Kone kone jata lukano andhar milave dhanya haye.
Tomari punya aloke basiya sabare basibo bhalo.
Parashmonir pradeep tomar, achapal tar alo –
Sona kare labe palake amar sakal kalanka kalo,
Ami jata deep jwaliachhi tahe sudhu jwala, sudhu kali –
Amar gharer duare shiyare tomari kiran dhale.

With thy own hands enkindle the lamp in my room.
Let all sorrow and bereavement be fruitful by
being blessed with thy light.
All darkness in every nook and corner would disappear in
blessings,
Sitting in thy auspicious halo I would love one and all.
Thy lamp is of touching gem, *sans* restlessness is its light
All my dark scars would in a moment be turned into gold.
Whate'er lamp have I brimmed is full of burns and dirt
Shower thy lustre beside the bed in the doors of my room.

☆☆☆

(100)

Tumi je esechho mor bhavane rab uthechhe bhuvane.
Nahile phoole kisher rang legechhe, gagane kon gaan jegechhe,
kon parimal pavane.
Diye duhkhasukher vedona amay tomar sadhana.
Amar vyethay vyethay pa pheliya ele tomar sur meliya,
Ele amar jeevane.

That thou hast come to my residence the sound is surging all
thro' the world
Else what colour has adorned the flowers which song is there
in the sky
Which fragrance fabricates the wind.
With achings of happiness and sorrow inflicted upon me
thy meditation begins
Stepping on my pains and pains, thou hast come spreading
thy tunes.
Thou hast come in my life.

☆☆☆

(101)

Apnake ei jana amar phoorabe na.
Ei janari sange sange tomay chena.
Kata janam-maranete tomari ei charanete
Apnake je debo, tabu barbe dena.
Amare je namte habe ghate ghate
Bare bare ei bhubaner praner hate
Vyevsa mor tomar sathe chalbe bere dine rate.
Apna niye karbo jatoi becha kena.

This knowing of the self will on my part never end.
With this very knowing I recognise thee.
In so many births and deaths at those feet of thine
Shall I submit, yet debts would increase.
I will have to plunge on every shore
Time and again in the assembly of life in this world.
My business is with thee by day and night would
go on increasing
At per with self-transaction.

☆☆☆

(102)

Aji nirbhaya nidrita bhuvane jage, ke jage,
Ghana sourabhamanthara pavane jage, ke jage.
Kata nirav vihangakulaye
Mohan anguli bulaye – jage, ke jage.
Kata asphoota pusper gopane jage, ke jage.
Ei apar ambarpathare
Stambhita gambhira andhare – jage, ke jage.
Mamo gabhir antar vedane jage, ke jage.

Who awakes today in the fearlessly asleep world.
Who awakes in the wind slow in fragrance?
With the touch of fine fingers in the limitless
silent nest of birds.
Who awakes?
With the privacy of unbloomed flowers in legion
Who awakes?
In this unending sea of clouds
Amidst startled and serene darkness
Who awakes?
In my poignant pain of the heart
Who awakes?

☆☆☆

(103)

E je mor avaran
Ghuchate katakshan.
Nishwasbaay ure chale jaay
Tumi karo jadi mon.
Jadi pare thaki bhume
Dhular dharani chume,
Tumi tari lagi dware rabe jaagi
E kemon taba pon.
Rather chakar rabe
Jagao jagao sabe,
Apanar ghare eso balabhare
Eso eso gourave.
Ghoom tute jaak chale,
Chini jeno Prabhu bale–
Chhute ese dware kari apanare
Charane samarpon.

This is my veil
How long to wipe it off.
The breathing wind flies away
If thou art interested
If on the ground do I remain
Kissing the dusty earth
For that very purpose thou wouldst remain awake on the door
What a promise is this on thy part?
With the sound of the wheels of the chariot
Awake, awake one and all.
In thy own room come forcibly,
Come, come in glory
Let slumber be away
Let me recognise thee as the Lord
Rushing towards the door do I submit
At thy feet.

☆☆☆

(104)

Eto alo jwaliechhe ei gagane
Kee utsaver lagane.
Sab aloti kemon kare phelo amar mukher pare
Apni thake alor pichchane.
Premti jedin jwali hriday-gagane
Kee utsaver lagane
Sab alo tar kemon kare pare tomar mukher pare
Apni pari alor pichhane.

So much light hast thou enkindled in this sky
at the time of the ceremony I know not.
How dost thou expose the whole light on my countenance
And thou dost remain behind the light.
When I trim on love in the sky of the heart
at the time of the ceremony I know not
How all light it exposed on thy countenance
And I remain behind the light.

☆☆☆

(105)

Amay bhulte dite naiko tomar bhay.
Amar bholar achhe anta, tomar premer to nai kshay
Dure giye barai je ghoor, se dur sudhu amari dur —
Tomar kachhe dur kabhu dur noy.

Amar praner kunri papri nahi khole,
Tomar vasantabay nai ki go tai bale.
Ei khelate amar sane har mano je kshane kshane —
Harer majhe achhe tomar joy.

No fear hast thee to allow me to forget.
There is limit to my forgetting, thy love knows no destruction
Going away, I simply increase the distance, that distance is mine alone —
To thee distance is never so.

The bud of my life does not unfold her petals.
Does it mean that there is no springtime wind for thee?
In this game with me at every time dost thou accept defeat.
Amidst that defeat thy victory lies.

☆☆☆

(106)

Amar vani amar prane lage –
Jata tomay daki, amar apon hriday jage.
Sudhu tomar chaoa seo amar paoa,
Tai to paran paranpane haat bariye mage.
Hay asakta, bhaye thakish pichhe.
Lagle sebay asakti tor apni habe michhe.
Path dekhabar tare jabo kahar ghare –
Jemni ami chali, tomar pradip chale age.

My message touches my heart –
The more I call on thee, the more does my heart awake.
Thy wants alone are also my receipts
So my life frantically prays for thy offerings.
O weak, in fear do ye remain behind
Thro' service your weakness would by itself be false.
In whose room shall I go to show the way
As I traverse, thy lamp precedes.

☆☆☆

(107)

Nibir ghana andhare jwalichhe dhrubatara.
Mon re mor, pathare hos ne dishehara.
Bishade hoye mriyaman bandha na kariyo gaan,
Saphal kari tolo pran tutiya mohakara.
Rakhiyo bal jeevane, rakhiyo chĩra-asha,
Shovan ei bhuvane rakhiyo bhalobasa.
Sangsarer sukhe dukhe chaliya jeyo hasimukhe,
Bhariya sada rekho booke tahari sudhadhara.

Amidst deep dense darkness the polestar is burning.
O my mind, do not lose direction in the sea.
Being distressed in grief stop not your music
Turn life into a success by breaking off the prison of enchantment.
Have strength in life, keep hope for eternity
Enrich this beautiful world with love.
In the weal and woe of the world, bid farewell in a happy countenance.
Always fill in the breast with his very stream of juice.

☆☆☆

(108)

Gabhir rajani namilo hridaye, ar kolahal nai.
Rahi rahi sudhu sudur sindhur dhwani sunibare pai.
Sakal basana chitte elo phire, nivir andhar ghanalo vahire –
Pradip ekti nibhrita antare jwalitechhe ek dhain.
Asim mangale mililo madhuri, khela halo samadhan.
Chapal chanchal laharilila paravare avasan.
Nirav mantre hriday majhe santi santi santi vaje.
Arupkanti nirakhi antare mudritulochane chai.

The poignant night descended in the heart, no more noise is there.
At time the sound of the distant sea alone do I hear.
All desires came back to the mind, dense darkness consolidated
outside –
In the secluded mind a lamp is continually burning.
Sweetness was in unison with endless auspiciousness,
play came to an end
The play of waves frivolous and restless ends in the sea.
In silent *mantras* amidst the heart peace continually rings.
The exquisite appearance do I behold in the mind and in
closed eyes do I look.

☆☆☆

(109)

Kee sur vaje amar prane ami-i jani, mani-jane.
Kiser lagi sadai jagi, kahar kachhe kee dhan magi –
Takai keno pather pane.
Dwarer pase prabhat ase, sandhya name vaner vame.
Sakal-sanjhe vanshi vaje, vikal kare sakal kaje –
Vajay ke je kisher tane.

It is I who knows, my mind alone knows what tune plays on
in my life –
Why I awake all the time, what wealth do I pray for,
and to whom.
Why do I feast my eyes towards the path.
Morning comes beside the door, evening plunges towards the
left of the forest.
The flute plays on from morn till evening makes idle in
all work
Ah, who plays on and in which tune!

☆ ☆ ☆

(110)

Tumi je amare chao ami se jani.
Keno je more kandao ami se jani.
E aloke e andhare keno tumi apanare
Chhayakhani diye chhao ami se jani.
Saradin nana kaje keno tumi nana saje
Kata sure daak dao ami se jani.
Sara hale deya-neya dinanter sesh kheya
Kon-dik-pane vao ami se jani.

I know that you want me.
I know why you make me weep.
In this light and darkness why you cover yourself
With your own shadow, I know that.
All day in various activities why in diverse dresses
You call on in different tunes, I know that.
When the last crossing at day's end is over in transaction
The direction of your rowing do I know.

☆☆☆

(111)

Charandhwani suni taba, Nath, jeevanteere
Kata neerav nirjane kata madhu samire.
Gagane grahatarachay animeshe chahi roy,
Bhavenasrot hridaye boy dhire ekante dhire.
Chahiya rahe ankhi mamo trishnatur pakhisamo,
Sravon royechhi meli chittagabhire —
Kon subhaprate danrave hridimajhe,
Bhulibo sab dukkha sukh dubiya anandaneere.

On the shores of life, O Lord, I listen to the sounds of
thy feet.
In lonely silence and gentle breeze in abundance.
The planets and the stars in the sky remain
gazing all along
The currents of thoughts flow on slowly, very slowly,
in the heart
Like thirsty birds do my eyes remain staring
In the depth of the mind have I spread my ears.
On what auspicious morn thou wouldst stand
amidst my heart
Drowning in joyous water I shall forget all sorrow
and happiness.

☆☆☆

(112)

Ananderi sagar hate esechhe aaj baan.
Dar dhare aaj bosh re sabai, taan re sabai taan.
Bojha jatai bojhai kari karbo re paar dukher tari,
  Dheuer 'pare dharbo pari — jaay jadi jaak pran.
Ke dake re pichhan hate, ke kare re mana,
Bhayer katha ke bale aaj — bhay achhe sab jana.
Kon shape kon graher doshe sukher dangay thakbo base.
  Paler rashi dharbo kashi, chalbo geye gaan.

Tide has come from the very sea of joy
O all be seated today holding oars, pull on,
  O all pull on.
With all burdens slacked we would cross the
  boat of sorrow
On the waves shall we cross be it with our death.
Who calls from behind, who forbids
Who speaks about fear today — every fear is known.
For which curse and fault of the planets should we
  remain seated on the land of happiness.
Strongly would we catch hold of the string of the sail
  and go on singing.

☆☆☆

(113)

Rajarajendra joy, joyotu joy he.
Byepta partap taba viswamoy he.
Dustadaldalan taba danda bhoykari, satrujandarpahara dipta tarabari –
Sankatsaranya tumi dainyadukhhari
Mukta-abarodh taba abhyuday he.

Hail, King of kings, victory, victory to thee,
Thy power is spread all o'er the universe.
Thy punishment to maul the band of the wicked is fearful
Thy sword is shining with the elimination of the pride of enemies
A solace in crisis, thou art the remover of poverty and sufferings
Thy barriers are free, O the Awakener.

☆☆☆

(114)

Jagrata viswa-kolahal-majhe
Tumi gambhir, stabdha, santa, nirbikar,
Paripurna mahajnan.
Toma-pane dhay pran sab kolahal chhari,
Chanchal nadi jemon dhay sagare.

Amidst the awakening noise of the universe
Thou art serene, silent, calm, *sans* reaction
Total erudition in legion.
Life rushes towards thee leaving all noise
As a restless river rushes towards the sea.

☆☆☆

(115)

Jagite habe re—
Mohanidra kabhu na rabe chiradin,
Tyejite haibe sukhshayan asanighosane.
Jage tar nyaydanda sarvabhuvane,
Phire tar kalchakra asim gagane,
Jwale tar rudranetra paaptimire.

O, we'd have to wake
The enchanted sleep won't last for ever,
The happy bed would have to be given up in
electrifying call
His scale of justice exists all o'er the world,
His wheel of Time moves in the endless sky,
His furious eyes burn in the darkness of sin.

☆ ☆ ☆

(116)

Ekhono tare chokhe dekhi ni, sudhu vanshi sunechhi –
Mon pran jaha chhilo diye phelechhi.
Sunechhi murati kalo tare na dekhai bhalo,
Sakhi, balo ami jal anite Jamunay jabo ki.
Sudhu swapane esechhilo se, nayankone hesechhilo se.
Se abadhi soi, bhaye bhaye roi – ankhi melite bheve sara hoi
Kanonpathe je khushi se jay, kadamtale je khusi she chaay –
Sakhi, balo ami ankhi tule karo pane chabo ki.
Sakhi, ami ankhi tule karo pane chabo ki.

Till now did I not see him in eyes, only his flute have I heard.
I've offered the mind and the heart and everything I had.
I've heard that his image is black, it's better not to see him
Friend, tell me if I'd go to *Yamuna* to fetch water
In dreams alone did he come, in the corner of the eyes did he laugh.
From that onward, friend, do I remain in fear –
I find no end of my thought to open my eyes.
Anyone desirous goes by the path of the flower garden,
anyone willing winks at beneath the *Kadam* tree
Friend, tell if I with eyes up look at anyone.
Friend, shall I with eyes up look at anyone.

☆☆☆

(117)

Hridaymandire pranadhish, achho gopane.
Amritasourabhe akul pran, hay,
Bhramiya jugate na pay sandhan —
Ke pare pasite anadabhavane
Tomar karunakiron-vihane.

In the temple of the heart, Lord of life, thou dost
remain in secret.
Alas, the enamoured life in the fragrance of nectar
Roam in the world but fails to trace out —
Who can behold in the mansion of joy
Sans thy light of pity?

☆☆☆

(118)

Shon re shon abodh mon,
Shon sadhur ukti, kise mukti sei sujukti kar grahan.
Bhaver shukti bhenge muktimukto kar anvesan,
Ore o bhola mon.

Listen, O listen, the unrealising mind
Listen to the statement of saints, accept that good advice
on which emancipation depends
Breaking the oyster of the world, seek the pearl of
emancipation
O the forgetful mind.

☆☆☆

(119)

Sunya pran kande sada — praneswar,
Deenabandhu, dayasindhu,
Prembindu katare karo daan.
Karo na sakha, karona
Chiranishphal ei jeevan.
Prabhu, janame marane tumi gati
Charane dao sthan.

Lord of life, the vacant life always weeps,
O Friend of the poor, sea of kindness
To the distressed contribute drops of love,
Don't O Friend, don't make this life fruitless for ever.
Lord, thou art the solace in life and death
Allow me to have my seat at thy feet.

☆☆☆

(120)

Oi pohalo timir rati,
Purvagagane dekha dilo nava prabhatchhata.
Jeevane jouvane hridaye vahire
Prakashila ati aparup madhur bhati.
Ke pathalo e shubhodin nidra-majhe,
Maha mahollase jagaile charachar,
Sumangal asirvad varasile
Kari prachar sukhavarata —
Tumi chira sather sathi.

Yonder dawned the dark night
A new aura of light appeared in the eastern sky
In life and youth, in the heart and outside
A very exquisite and pleasing morn did spring forth.
Who sent this auspicious day amidst slumber,
In great hilarious cry did awaken the world,
Showered auspicious blessings
By spreading the message of happiness.
Thou art the comrade of eternal companionship.

(121)

Ami ekla chalechhi e bhave,
Amay pather sandhan ke kabe.
Bhay nei bhay nei –
Jao apon monei
Jemon ekla madhup dheye jay
Keval phooler sourabhe.

Alone have I walked on in this world
Who would tell me the source for my path
Fear not, no fear
Depart in your own mind
Just as the lone butterfly rushes on
Towards the fragrance of flowers alone.

☆☆☆

(122)

Ogo purovasi,
Ami dware danriye achhi upavasi.
Heritechhi sukhamela ghare ghare kata khela
Sunitechhi sara bela sumadhur vanshi.
Chahi na anek dhan, rabo na adhik kshan,
Jetha hate asiachhi setha jabo bhasi.
Tomara anande rabe nava nava utsave,
Kichhu mlan nahi habe grihabhara hasi.

O residents of interior houses
On the doors I've remained standing on fasting
The fair of happiness am I seeing, so many games
are going on in every room
All day long am I listening to the very pleasing flute.

Much wealth I want not, I won't stay for long
I would float away to the place wherefrom I've come
In joy you'd remain in newer ceremonies
The smile flooded in rooms won't for a bit be faded.

☆☆☆

(123)

Anek diyechho Nath,
Amar vasana tabu purilo na –
Deenadasha ghuchilo na, asruvari muchhilo na
Gabhir praner trisa mitila na, mitila na.
Dieychha jeevan mon, pranapriya parijan,
Sudhasnigdha samiran, neelkanta ambar, shyamashobha
dharani.
Eto jadi dile sakha, aro dite habe he –
Tomare na pele ami phiribo na, phiribo na.

Much have you given, Lord
Yet my desires did not fill in.
The poor condition waded not, tears wiped not
The thirst of the poignant life quenched not,
did not quench.
You've given life and mind, life-endearing relatives
Pleasant breeze, blue sky, green splashed world
Friend, if you've given so much, you'd have to
give more –
Sans you, I won't return, won't return.

☆☆☆

(124)

Peyechhi sandhan taba Antaryami, antare dekhechhi tomare,
Chakite chapal aloke, hriday satadalmajhe,
Herinu e kee aparup rup.
Kotha phiritechhilum pathe pathe dware dware –
Matiya kalarabe –
Sahasa kolahalmajhe sunechhi taba ahavan,
Nibhritahridaymajhe
Madhur gabhir santo vani

O Lord of Inwardness, I've got thy trace, I've seen you
amidst the mind
Within a moment in restless light, amidst the lotus
of the heart.
What an exquisite beauty did I behold!
Where on ways did I wander from door to door
intoxicating myself in noise
All on a sudden have I listened amid noise to
thy call,
In the secluded heart
The message pleasing serene calm.

☆☆☆

(125)

Dhara diyechhi go ami akasher pakhi,
Nayane dekhechhi taba nutan akash.
Dukhani ankhir pate kee rekhechho dhaki,
Hasile phootiya pare ushar abhash.
Hriday urite chay kothay ekaki —
Ankhitarakar deshe karibare bash.
Oi gaganete cheye uthiyachhe daki —
Hothay harate chay e geet-uchchhwas.

O submitted have I, the bird of the sky.
In your eyes have I seen the new sky
What have you wrapped up with the petals of two eyes.
Dawn blooms with your smile
Yonder the heart wants to fly alone
To live in the land of the stars of eyes.
Looking at that sky it has called out —
This overflow of songs wants to be lost there.

☆☆☆

(126)

Tomar dekha pabo bole esechhi-je sakha!
Shuno priyotamo he, kotha achho lukaiye —
Taba gopan bijon grihe laye jaao.
Deho go saraye tapan taraka
Aboron sab dur karo he, mochan karo timir —
Jagat-arale theko na birale,
Lukayo na aponari mahima-majhe —
Tomar griher dwar khule dao.

Friend, I've come only to encounter thee.
Listen O dearest, where art thou in concealment
Take me to thy secret lonely room
O remove the sun and the stars
O drive away all veils, wipe off darkness —
In the backdrop of the world, do not remain in loneliness
Hide not amidst thy own grandeur —
Open the doors of thy room.

☆☆☆

(127)

Tomari madhur rupe bharechhe bhubon —
Mugdha nayan mamo, pulakita mohit mon.
Tarun arun nabin bhati, purnimaprasanna rati,
Ruprashi-vikashito-tanu kusumavan.
Toma-pane chahi sakale sundar
Rup heri akul antar.
Tomare gheriya phire nirantar tomar prem chahi.
Uthe sangeet tomar pane, gagan purna premgaane
Tomar charan karechhe varan nikhiljan.

With thy pleasant beauty, the world is filled up —
Pleased are my eyes, joyful and enamoured is my mind.
The young sun is with his new lustre, the night is with
full-moon gladness.
The forest of flowers is with limbs of bloomed array of
beauty
Looking at thee everyone is beautiful,
Beholding thy beauty the heart is overflooded,
Encompassing thee, it continually haunts seeking thy love.
Music surges on towards thee, the sky is full of songs of love
The people of the world has welcomed thy feet.

☆☆☆

(128)

Amar prane gabhir gopan
Maha-apon se ki?
Andhakare hathat tare dekhi
Pagal haoar jhare
Agal khule pare
Kar se nayan-pare
Nayan jaay je theki.
Jakhan ase param lagan
Takhan gagan majhe
Tahar vanshi vaje.

Takhan amar gaane
Tahari sur ane,
Amontraner vani
Jaay hridaye lekhi.

In my heart serene and poignant
Is he the great endearing?
Suddenly do I behold him in darkness
In the storm of the mad wind
All barriers tumble down
On whose eyes
The eyes as if are arrested!
When the serene moment comes,
Then amid the sky
His flute plays on

Then in my song
His very song brings forth his tune
The message of welcome
On the heart is written.

☆☆☆

(129)

Emon aar katadin chale jabe re!
Jeevaner bhar vahibo kato! Haay haay!
Je asha mone chhilo, sakali phoorailo —
Kichhu halo na jeevane.
Jeevan phooraye elo. Haay haay!

O how many more days like this would pass away,
How long would I bear the burden of life!
Alas, alas!
The hope that brimmed in the mind did all
come to an end
Nothing happened to be of use in life.
Life came to an end. Alas, alas!

☆☆☆

(130)

Ami deen ati deen –
Kemone sudhibo, Nath he, taba karunarin.
Taba sneho sata dhare dubaichhe sangsare,
Tapito hridaymajhe jharichhe nishidin.
Hridaye ja achhe dibo taba kachhe,
Tomari e prem dibo tomare –
Chiradin taba kaje rahibo jagatmajhe,
Jeeven karechhi tomar charantale leen.

Poor am I, very poor –
How shall I, O Lord, repay thy debt of pity!
In a hundred streams thy affection has dipped
the world
Amidst the heated heart is it sprinkling day and
night.
Whate'er is there in the heart would I deliver to thee
To thee would I offer this love of thine.
In the service would I ever remain in the world
At thy feet have I sacrificed this life.

☆☆☆

(131)

Sunechhe tomar nam anath atur jan –
Esechhe tomar dware, sunya phere na jena.
Kande jara nirashay ankhi jena muchhe jaay
Jena go abhay paay trase kampita mon.
Kata sata achhe deen abhaga aloyheen,
Shoke jeerna pran kata kanditechhe nisidin.
Paape jara dubiyachhe jabe tara kar kachhe –
Kotha hay path achhe, dao taro darasan.

The orphan and the distressed have heard thy name.
They've come to thy door, let them not return in emptiness.
Let the eyes of those crying in hopelessness be mopped up
O let the mind trembling in fear be blessed with fearlessness.
So many hundreds of people are there poor hapless homeless
So many hearts are there tattered in bereavement
weeping day and night.
To whom would those drowned in vice take refuge
Alas, where's the way, bless them with thy appearance.

☆☆☆

(132)

Sono tar sudhavani subhomuhurte santoprane –
Chharo chharo kolahal, chharo re apon katha,
Akashe divanishi uthale sangeet dhwani tahar,
Ke sune se madhu veenarav –
Adhir visva sunyapathe halo vahir.

Listen to His pleasing message on the auspicious moment
in a quiet heart
Leave, leave all noise, O leave all words of the self.
Day and night the sound of His music o'erfloods in the sky
Who listens to that sweet sound of the *veena*
The restless universe came out in the vacant path.

☆☆☆

(133)

Amar nisithrater badaldhara eso he gopane
Amar swapanloke dishahara.
Ogo andhakarer antardhan, dao dheke mor paran mon –
Ami chai ne tapan, chai ne tara,
Jakhan sabai magan ghoomer ghore niyo go, niyo go,
Amar ghoom niyo go haran kare.
Amar ekla ghare chupe chupe eso keval surer rupe –
Diyo go, diyo go
Amar chokher jaler diye sara.

O streams of rain at midnight, come stealthily
In my world of dreams *sans* direction.
O the inward wealth of darkness, cover up my life
and mind –
The sun or the stars I want not either
When all are rapt in slumber,
Steal O steal my slumber away
In my single room come silently
in the form of tune only
Give, O give
Response to my tears.

☆☆☆

(134)

Jakhan dekha dao ni Radha, takhan vejechhilo vanshi.
Ekhon chokhe chokhe cheye sur je amar gelo bhasi.
Takhan nana taner chhale
Dak phirechhe jale sthale,
Ekhon amar sakal kanda Radhar rupe uthlo hasi.

When you, Radha, did not appear, the flute played on
Now looking at eyes my tune floated away
Then with diverse pretexts
The beckoning has travelled in land and water
Now all my weepings burst out laughing in the
beauty of Radha.

☆☆☆

(135)

Vadhur lagi keshe ami parvo emon phool
Swarge martye tin bhuvane naiko jahar mool.
Vanshir dhwani haoay bhase, sabar kane vajbe na she –
Dekh lo cheye Yamuna oi chhapiye gelo kool.

For the bride I'd dress my hair with such a flower
As would be priceless in the heaven, the earth, in
the three worlds.
In the wind the sound of the flute floats, it won't ring
in every ear.
O behold the yonder Yamuna o'erflooded the banks.

☆☆☆

(136)

Madhuritu nitya hoye railo tomar madhur deshe –
Jaoa-asar kannahasi haoay setha veray bhese.
Jaay je jana sei sudhu jaay, phool phota to phooray na haay –
Jharbe je phool sei kebali jhare pare velaseshe.
Jakhan ami chhilem kachhe takhan kata diyechhi gaan –
Ekhon amar dure jaoa, ero ki go nai kono daan.
Puspavaner chhayay dheke ei asha tai gelem rekhe –
Agun-bhara fagunke tor kanday jeno ashar ese.

In your pleasant land, the sweet season remained for ever
The laughter and tears of arrival and departure travel
there in the air afloating
One who departs departs alone, the blooming of flowers,
ah, never ends.
The flower about to wither withers alone at the end
of the day.
When I was nearer so many songs have I contributed—
Now is the time for me to go far, O, has it, too, no
contribution?
Covering in the shadow of the forest of flowers, this hope,
therefore, do I leave behind:
Let *Ashar* arrive and make your fire-filled *Fagoon* weep.

☆☆☆

(137)

Ogo santa pasanmurati sundari,
Chanchalere hridaytale lao bari,
Kunjavane eso eka, nayane asru dik dekha –
Arun rage hok ranjita vikasita vedanar vani.

O calm stone-image Beauty,
Accept the restless one in the core of your heart.
Come alone in the grove, let tears appear in eyes.
In the lustre of the sun let the buds of pains
be hallowed and effulged.

☆☆☆

(138)

Ami phool tulite elem vane—
Jani ne, amar kee chhilo mone.
E to phool tola noy, vujhi ne kee mone hoy,
Jal bhare jaay du nayane.

To the forest did I come to pluck flowers
Know not I what was there in my mind
This is not just picking up flowers, what
happens I do not realise
Tears well up in two eyes.

☆☆☆

(139)

Vijoymala eno amar lagi.
Dirgharatri raibo ami jagi.
Charan jakhan parbe tomar marankule
Vooker madhye uthbe amar Paran dule,
Sab jadi jaay habe tomar sarbanasher bhagi.

Bring the garland of victory for me
I would remain awake for long night.
When my feet would step on your shore of death
My heart would swing amidst my breast
If everything is gone, I'd be a partner to your disaster.

☆ ☆ ☆

(140)

Amar hariye-jaoa din
Aar ki khoonje pave tare
Badal diner akash-pare –
Chhayay halo leen.
Kon karun mukher chhabi
Puven haoay mele dilo
Sajal bhairavi.
Ei gahan vanachchhay
Anek kaler stabdhavani
Kahar apekshay
Achhe vachanhin.

My lost day –
Shall I trace it out any more
in the shore of the sky of rainy days
It is in unison with shadow.
Whose picture of pitiful countenance
The drenched *bharavi*
Spread in the eastern wind!
In this dense shadow of the forest
For whom does the silent message of
many times
Remain speechless?

☆☆☆

(141)

Navajeevaner yatrapathe dao dao ei bar
He hridayeshwar –
Premer bitta purna kariya dik chitta;
Jena e sangsarmajhe taba dakshinmukh raje;
Sukhrupe pai taba bhiksha, dukhrupe pai taba deeksha;
Mon hak kshudrata mukta, nikhiler sathe hok yukta,
Subhokarme jeno nahi mane klanti
Santi santi santi.

In the journey of new life, bless, bless with this boon,
O Lord of the heart.
Let the wealth of love fill in the mind.
As if in this world your positive look adorns
Your mercy do I receive in the form of happiness,
your initiation in that of sorrow
Let the mind be free from pettiness and in unison with
the world
Let no boredom be admitted in auspicious work
Peace peace peace.

☆☆☆

(142)

He nutan,
Dekha dik ar-bar jamer pratham subhakshan.
Tomar prakash hok kuhelika kari udghatan
suryer maton.
Riktatar vaksha bhedi aponare karo unmochan.
Vyekta hok jeevaner joy,
Vyekta hok toma-majhe asimer chira-vismoy.
Udaydigante sankho vaje, mor chittamajhe
Chiranutanere dilo dak
Panchise Vaisakh.

O New,
Let the first auspicious moment of birth reappear
Let your effulgence be made by moving the mirage
Like the sun.
Tearing off the breast of the void, open yourself.
Let the victory of life be expressed.
Let amidst you be expressed the eternal·wonder of the endless
The twenty-fifth day of *Vaisakh*
Beckons the Ever New.

☆☆☆

(143)

Oi mahamanav ase.
Dike dike romancha lage
Martyadhulir ghase ghase.
Suraloke beje othe sankho
Naraloke baje joydonko –
Elo mahajanmer lagna.
Aji amaratrir durgatoran jata
Dhulitale haye gelo bhagna.
Udayshikhare jage 'mabhai mabhai'
Navajeevaner aswashe
'Joy joy joy re manav-abhyuday'
Mandri uthilo mahakashe.

Yonder the Great Man comes
Thrills encompass every direction
Amid the dust and grass of the earth
Conchshells ring in the heaven
The drum of victory plays on in the world
The moment of great birth came
All the gates of the fortress of dark nights
Are crushed in the dust
'Fear not, be not afraid' hails in the rising peak
With the hope of new life.
'Victory, victory, O victory to the awakening of man'—
The space resounds.

☆☆☆

(144)

Nava anande jaago aji navaravikirane
Subhra sundar priti-ujjwal nirmal jeevane.
Utsarila nava jeevan nirjhar uchchhasita ashageeti,
Amrita puspagandha vahe aji ei santipavane.

With the light of the new sun awake today in joy anew
In life pure and lovely, loving and shining and clean
The new fountain of light is o'erflooded, the songs of hope
surging
In this air adorned with peace the fragrance of
nectar-like flowers flows.

☆☆☆

(145)

Aji e anandasandhya sundar vikase, aha,
Manda-pavane aji bhase akashe
Vidhur vyakul madhumaadhuri, aha,
Stavdha gagane grahatara nirave
Kiransangeete sudha varase, aha,
Pran man mamo dhire dhire prasadrase ase bhari
Deho pulakito udar harase, aha.

Ah, this joyous evening lovingly manifests
In the breeze today does effulge in the sky
The agonised restless sweet grandeur, ah.
In the silent sky, silently the planets and the stars
Shower the juice in the songs of light, ah.
My life and the mind are slowly filled in
with the juice of offerings.
Joyful is the body with the gracious smile, ah.

☆☆☆

(146)

Sada thaako anande, sangsare nirbhaye nirmalprane
Jago prate anande, karo karma anande,
Sandhay grihe chalo he anandagaane
Sankate sampade thako kalyane
Thako anande ninda-apamaane
Sabare kshama kari thaako anande
Chira-amrita nirjhare santiraspane.

Remain in joy all the time in the world
    fearless and with a heart pure
Awake in joy in the morning, work in joy,
In songs of joy return home in the evening.
Remain in goodness in crisis and affluence,
In disgrace and dishonour remain in joy,
In joy remain by pardoning all
In drinking peace in the fountain of nectar for ever.

☆☆☆

(147)

Hridayvasana purno halo aaji mama purno halo,
Suno save jagat jane
Kee herinu shobha, nikhilbhuvannath
Chitta-majhe vasi sthir asane.

Filled today is the desire of the heart, O filled today
Listen all the people of the world
What a sight did I see, O Lord of the universe.
Sitting on the constant seat in the midst of the mind.

☆☆☆

(148)

Vahe nirantar ananta anandadhara
Vaje asim nabhomajhe anadi rab,
Jage aganya ravichandratara.
Ekak akhanda brahmandarajye
Param-ek sei rajarajendra raje.
Vismito nimeshhata visva charane vinata
Lakshasata bhaktachita vakyahara.

The endless stream of joy continually flows.
Amid unending firmament the sound *sans*
beginning sings.
Countless sun the moon and the stars awake.
In the one undivided kingdom of the universe
Adorns that Supreme One, the King of the kings.
Agonised moment-struck drooped on the feet of
the world,
Hundreds and millions of the minds of the devotees are speechless.

☆☆☆

(149)

Anandagaan uthuk tabe vaji
Ebar amar vyathar vanshite,
Asrujaler dheuer 'pare aji
Parer tari thakuk bhasite.
Jabar haoa oi-je uthechhe, ogo, oi-je uthechhe,
Sararatri chakshe amar ghoom je chhutechhe.
Hriday amar uthechhe dule dule
Akul jaler attahasite —
Ke go tumi dao dekhi tan tule
Ebar amar vyathar vanshite.
He ajana, ajana sur nava
Vajao amar vyathar vanshite
Hathat ebar ujan haoay taba
Parer tari thak na bhasite.
Kona kale hoyni jare dekha ogo, tari virahe
Emon kare daak diyechhe — ghare ke rahe.
Basar asha giyechhe mor ghure,
Jhanp diyechhi akashrashite
Pagal, tomar sristichhara sure
Taan diye mor vyathar vanshite.

Let the song of joy ring in
Now in my painful flute
Let on the waves of tears now
The boat of the shore float on.
The wind for departure has surged yonder,
ye, yonder has surged
All night sleep has run along in my eyes.
My heart has swung up
In the bursting laughters of shoreless water —
Who ye are, please raise the tune
Now in my painful flute.
O unknown, tune on new unknown tunes
In my painful flute.

All of a sudden in the flowing wind
    Let the boat of the shore remain afloating.
Whom no encounter did ever allow to be, ye,
    With me, his languishment the beckoning has come —
                                who remains in the room?
My hope of a resident is turned
    In the profusion of the sky have I plunged
O Mad, in your tune out of creation
    Attune my painful flute.

☆☆☆

(150)

Andhar rajani pohalo jagat purilo pulake.
Vimal prabhat kirane mililo dyulok bhuloke.
Jagat nayan tulia hridayduar khulia
Herichhe hridaynathere apon hriday-aloke.
Premamukhakhani tanhari parichhe dharar anane —
Kusum vikoshi uthichhe, samir vahichhe kanane.
Sudhire andhar tutichhe, dash dik phoote utichhe —
Jananeer kole jeno re jagichhe valika valake.
Jagat je dike chahichhe se dike dekhinu chahiya,
Heri se aseem madhuri hriday uthichhe gahiya.
Navin aloke bhatichhe, navin ashay matichhe
Navin jeevan labhiya joy joy uthe triloke.

The dark night dawned; in joy was the world filled.
The pure morning sunlight made heaven in unison with the earth.
Raising the eyes and opening the door of the heart
The world is visualizing the Lord of the heart in his own light
of the heart.
His loving countenance on the mirror of the world
is reflecting,
Flowers are in bloom, the wind in the garden
is blowing
Darkness is very slowly being erased out, everywhere there is
awakening
In the lap of night as it were are boys and girls rising.
Eyeing at the direction where the world is beholding
I encountered endless beauty: the heart leaps up singing
In new light everything is shining in intoxication of new hope
Achieving new life the slogan of victory pervades everywhere.

☆☆☆

(151)

Oi amal haate rajani praate apni jwalo
Ei to alo — ei to alo,
Ei to prabhat, ei to akash, ei to pujar puspavikash,
Ei to vimal, ei to madhur, ei to bhalo —
Ei to alo — ei to alo.
Andhar megher vakshe jege apni jwalo
Ei to alo — ei to alo.
Ei to jhanjha tarit-jwala, ei to dukher agnimala,
Ei to mukti, ei to dipti, ei to bhalo —
Ei to alo — ei to alo.

In that serene hand in day and night enkindle yourself
This then is light — light just it is.
This then is morning, this then is the sky, the
efflorescence of flowers of offerings it just is
Serene this then is, pleasant just it is, this is just well —
This then is light — light just it is
Waking in the breast of dark cloud, enkindle yourself
This then is light — light just it is
This then is gale, the burning of lighting, the garland of
the fire of sorrow this just is
This then is emancipation, lustre this then is, this is just well —
This then is light — light just it is.

☆☆☆

(152)

Gaaye amar pulak laage, chokhe ghanaay ghor —
Hridaye mor ke vendhechhe ranga rakhir dor.
Ajike ei-akashtale jale sthale phoole phale
Kemon kare manoharan, chharale mon mor.
Kemon khela halo amar aji tomar sane!
Peyechhi ki khunje verai bheve na pai mone.
Ananda aj kiser chhale kandite chaay nayanjale,
Viraha aj madhur hoye karechhe pran bhor.

Joy embraces my body, illusion touches my eyes —
Who has fastened the coloured thread of *raakhi* in my heart!
Under this sky today, in land and water, flowers and fruits
How the enticer of mind has scattered my mind
What a play with you was there by me!
I go on seeking what I have received, my mind fails to think it over.
In what disguise joy today does want to weep in tears
Languishment is turned pleasant today and has dawned the mind.

☆☆☆

(153)

Prane khushir toofan uthechhe.
Bhoy-bhavonar vadha tutechhe.
Duhkhake aj kathin vale jarie dharte vuker tale
Udhao hoye hridoy chhutechhe.
Hethay karo thain habe na mone chhilo el bhabona,
Duar bhenge sabi jutechhe.
Jatan kare apnake je rekhechhilem dhuye meje
Anande se dhulay lutechhe.

The storm of joy has arisen in the mind.
The constraints of fear and agony are torn apart.
With sorrow clasped in great force under the breast,
The heart is running away to the unknown.
None would have a refuge here so was the thought
of the mind
Breaking open the door, everyone has assembled
The self whom I with care kept clean and brushed
Lies on the dust in joy.

☆☆☆

(154)

Eto anandadhwani uthilo kothay,
Jagatpurabasi sabe kothay dhaay.
Kon amritadhaner peyechhe sandhan,
Kon sudha kare paan.
Kon aloke andhar dure jaay.

Where did so much sound of joy arise
Where do the world-residents rush on
Of what wealth of nectar have they traced out
What drink do they enjoy
In which light does darkness depart?

☆☆☆

(155)

Kshata jata kshati tata michhe hate michhe,
Nimesher kushankur pari rabe niche.
Kee hala na, kee pele na, ke taba shodhe ni dena
Se sakali marichika milaibe pichhe
Ei-je herile chokhe aparup chhabi
Arun gagantale prabhater rabi —
Ei to param daan safal karila pran
Satyer anandaroop
Ei to jagichhe.

As there are wounds so are the losses,
from falsehood to falsehood
The grass-bud of the moment will lag behind.
What was not made, what not received, who repaid
not the debt
Mirage as all these are will afterwards disappear
This exquisite picture that you just beheld —
The morning sun in the red sky —
This is the great gift that made the lift successful
As the joy of Truth
Is this waking just now.

☆☆☆

(156)

Vipul taranga re vipul taranga re
Sab gagan udvelia — magan kari ateet anagata.
Aloke ujjwal jeevane chanchal eki ananda-taranga.
Tai, dulichhe dinakar chandra tara,
Chamaki kampichhe chetanadhara
Akul chanchal nache sangsar, kuhare hridayvihanga.

Vast are the waves, O vast are the waves
Surpassing all the sky, submerging the past and
the future
What waves of joy bright in light and restless in life
So, the sun and the moon and the stars
are swinging
The stream of consciousness is trembling with a flash
The world totally restless dances, the bird
of the heart twitters.

☆☆☆

(157)

Preme prane gaane gandhe aloke pulake
Plabito karia nikhil dyulok bhuloke
Tomar amal amrita parichhe jharia.
Dike dike aji tutia sakal bandha
Murati dharia jagia uthe ananda,
Jeevan uthilo nivir sudhay bharia.
Chetona amar kalyan-ras-sarase
Satadalsama phootilo param harase
Sab madhu tar charane tomar dharia.

In love and life, songs and smelling, light and joy
Flooding the universe, the heaven and the earth
Your pure nectar is falling in shower
In every direction by tearing off all constraints
Joy awakens by taking its image
Life is filled in with poignant drinks.
My consciousness drowned with the juice of goodness
Like a lily in bloom with great gladness
With all its honey at your feet.
In silent light on the edge of the heart
The red aura of awakening of the widened dawn arose
The veil of idle eyes removed.

☆☆☆

(158)

E din aji kon ghare go khule dilo dwar
Aji prate surya otha safal halo kaar.
Kahar abhiseker tare sonar ghate alok bhare
Usha kahar ashish vahi halo andhar paar.
Vane vane phool phootechhe, dole navin pata –
Kar hridayer majhe halo tader mala gantha.
Vahu juger upahare varan kari nilo tare
Kaar jeevane prabhat aji ghochay andhakar.

O in which room this day has opened the doors
today
To whom is today's sunrise in the morning
a success?
For whose coronation by filling in light in
the golden vase
The Dawn crossed darkness with the blessings
unknown
Flowers are in bloom at every forest, new leaves swing –
Amid whose heart is their garland entwined?
Who was welcomed with the gifts of many eras?
In whose life does morning eliminate darkness?

☆☆☆

(159)

Tar anta nai go je anande gara amar anga.
Tar anu-paramanu pelo kato alor sanga,
O tar anta nai go nai.
Tare mohanmantra diye gechhe kato phooler gandha
Tare dola diye dulie gechhe kato dheuer chhanda,
O tar anta nai go nai.
Achhe kato surer sohag je tar stare stare lagna,
Se je kato ranger rasadharay katoi halo magna,
O tar anta nai go nai.
Kato suktara je swapne tahar rekhe gechhe sparsa,
Kato vasanta je dhelechhe tay akaraner harsa,
O tar anta nai go nai.
Se je pran peyechhe pan kare jug-jugantarer stanya –
Bhubon kato teerthajaler dharay karechhe tay dhanya,
O tar anta nai go nai.
Se je sangini mor, amare se diyechhe varmalya
Ami dhanya, se mor angane je kato pradip jwallo –
O tar anta nai go nai.

O endless is the joy with which my limbs are built
Its molecules and atoms are blessed with the unending
companionship of light.

O no, no end it has.
Innumerable fragrance of flowers has christened him
with lovely chantings

So many rhythms of waves have cradled him
O no, no end it has.
The affection of innumerable tunes is ingrained in its
every stage

So much immersed it is with so many juicy streams
of colours.

O no, no end it has.
So many touches are left behind by the morning star
in dreams.

So many reasonless laughters are poured by the spring
upon these.
O no, no end it has.
He has regained life by sucking the breast of
age beyond age
With the stream of water from so many pilgrim —
places the world has glorified him,
O no, no end it has.
A companion she is to me, and as a husband
has garlanded me.
Glorified am I, so many lamps has she enkindled
in my courtyard
O no, no end it has.

☆☆☆

(160)

Anandadhara vahichhe bhavane,
Dinarajani kata amritaras uthali jaay ananta gagane.
Paan kare rabi sashi anjali bharia –
Sada deepto rahe akshay jyoti –
Nitya purna dhara jeevane kirane.
Vasia achho keno apon-mane,
Swarthanimagan kee karane?
Chari dike dekho chahi hriday prasari,
Kshudra duhkha sab tuchchha mani
Prem bharia laho sunyo jeevane.

The stream of joy is flowing in the world
In what a profusion is the nectar-flow overflows
the unending sky
With folded palms the sun and the moon
drink,
The everlasting aura remains ever enlightened
With light in life the earth is eternally filled.
Why seated alone in your mind,
Why immersed in the self?
Look around with an expanded heart,
Considering all petty sorrow to be insignificant
Fill in with love the empty life.

☆☆☆

(161)

Jagate anandajajne amar nimantran.
Dhanya halo, dhanya halo manavjeevan.
Nayan amar rooper poore sadh mitaye varay ghure,
Shravan amar gabhir sure hoyechhe magan.
Tomar jajne diyechho bhar, vajai ami vanshi —
Gaane gaane genthe verai praner kanna hasi
Ekhon samoy hoyechhe ki? Sabhay giye tomay dekhi
Joyodhwani sunie jabo emor nivedan.

In the feast of the world am I invited
Glory, glory it was for the human life.
In the kingdom of Beauty my eyes roam about fulfilling
all desires
My ears are rapt in poignant tunes.
I am assigned to your ceremony, on do I play the flute
In songs do I sew on the laughter and tears of the
heart
Is the time ripe now? Attending the meeting do I
behold you.
I'd depart making you listen to the sound of victory —
this is my submission.

☆☆☆

(162)

Parbi na ki jog dite ei chhande re
Khase jabar, bhese jabar, bhangbari anande re.
Patia kaan sunish na je dike dike gagan-majhe
Maranveenay kee sur vaje tapan-tara-chandre re —
Jwalie agoon dheye dheye jwalbari anande re.
Pagal-kara gaaner tane dhay je kotha kei ba jaane,
Chaay na phire pichhan-pane, roy no badha bandhe re —
Lootbe jabar, chhute jabar, chalbari anande re.
Sei ananda-charan-pate chhay ritu je nritye maate,
Plabon bahe jaay dharate baran geete gandhe re —
Phele debar, chhere debar, marbari anande re.

O would you be able to join this rhythm
In the joy of being dropped, floated away and,
of course, being broken
With ears alert you listen not that amid the sky
at every direction
What tune in the *veena* of death plays on the
sky and the stars and the moon —
By enkindling the fire in the joy of being burnt
in a rush
No one knows where he rushes on in the tune of
the intoxicating song
Behind he looks not, nor does the remain in cares
and constraints.
With the very joy of being enraptured, rushed on or moved
In that joyous setting of feet the six seasons are absorbed in
dancing
The flood sweeps on the world with the efflorescence of
the song of invocation
In the joy of dropping, leaving or dying.

☆☆☆

(163)

Tomar ananda oi elo dware, elo elo elo go, ogo purabasi
Vooker anchalkhani dhulay pete anginate melo go.
Pathe sechon karo gandhavari malin na hoi charan tari
Tomar sundar oi elo dware, elo elo elo go.
Akul hridaykhani sammukhe tar chhariye phelo phelo go.
Tomar sakal dhan je dhanya halo halo go.
Visvajaner kalyane aj gharer duar kholo go
Here ranga halo sakal gagan, chitto halo pulak-magan,
Tomar nitya alo elo dware, elo elo elo go
Tomar paran-pradip tule dharo, oi alote jwelo go.

Yonder at the door does your joy arrive, O indweller,
Placing the dress-end of the breast of the dust,
spread o'er the courtyard.
Fragrant water on the way sprinkle, let his feet be not dirty
On the doorsteps does your Beautiful come, O come.
Spread your restless heart before him
All your treasures have been glorified, O glorified
Open the doors of the room today for the
good of the people of the universe
Behold all the sky turned colourful, immersed in joy
was the mind.
Your eternal Light has come to the door, come O
come.
Lift your lamp of life, O enkindle with that light.

☆☆☆

(164)

Aloy alokmoy kare he ele alor alo.
Amar nayan hate andhar milalo milalo.
Sakal akash sakal dhara anande hasite bhara,
Je-dik pane nayan meli bhalo sabi bhalo.
Tomar alo gachcher patay nachiye tole pran.
Tomar alo pakhir basay jagiye tole gaan.
Tomar alo bhalobeshe parechhe mor gaye ese,
Hridaye mor nirmal haat bulalo bulalo.

Thou hast come, O Light of light, flooding with light
Darkness from my eyes disappeared.
All the sky and the world are full of joy and laughter,
Where'er do I feast my eyes, everything is well.
Thy light dancing makes leaves of trees dancing with life
Thy light arouses songs in the nests of birds.
Thy light has lovingly fallen on my body
Thy clear hands soothed my heart.

☆☆☆

(165)

Vaje vaje ramyaveena vaje –
Amal kamal-majhe, jyotsnarajani-majhe,
Kajalghana-majhe, nishi-andhar-majhe,
Kusumsurabhi-majhe, veenranan suni je –
Preme preme vaje.
Nache nache ramyatale nache –
Tapan tara nache, nadi samudra nache
Janmamaran nache, jugjuganta nache,
Bhakatahriday nache visvachhande matiye –
Preme preme nache.
Saje saje ramyabeshe saje –
Neel ambar saje, ushasandhya saje,
Dharanidhuli saje, deenaduhkhi saje,
Pranata chitte saje visva shobhay lutaye –
Preme preme saje.

The lovely *veena* plays on and on
Amid the beautiful lotus, the floodlit night,
In the deep dense black amid the darkness of night
In the fragrance of flowers the resonance of the *veena* do I listen
Playing on in love and love.
In lovely strokes dance on and on –
The sun and the stars dance, the rivers and the sea dance
Dance life and death, the age and the age beyond
The heart of the worshipper does dance intoxicating in the rhythm of the universe
Dance in love and love.
In lovely attires do dress on and on
The blue sky dresses, the dawn and the evening dress
The dust of the earth does dress, the poor and distressed dress
In revered mind dresses by endearing with the beauty of the universe
Dress in love and love.

☆☆☆

(166)

Amal kamal sahaje jaler kole anande rahe phutiya,
Phire na se kabhu 'aloy kothay' bale dhulay dhulay lutiya.
Temni sahaje anande harasita
Tomar majhare rabo nimagnachita,
Pujasatadal apani se vikasita sab sangshay tutiya.
Kotha achho tumi path na khunjivo kabhu, sadhavo na kono pathike —
Tomari majhare bhramibo phiribo Prabhu, jakhan phiribe jedike
Chalibe jakhan tomar akashgehe
Tomar amritaprabaha lagibe dehe,
Tomar paban sakhar matan snehe vakshe asibe chhutiya.

The serene lotus easily remains in joy in the lap of water
Never does it return by being prostrated on the
dust saying where is the residence
Delighted in the same way am I
Remain immersed in mind amidst thee
The lotus for worship is self-abloomed by dispelling
all doubts
Where thou art never whould I seek the path,
nor would I ask any traveller —
In the midst of thee alone would I wonder, my Lord,
when I would turn anyway.
When towards thy room in the sky would I move
Thy nectar-like current would touch my body
Like a friend with affection thy wind would rush forth
in the breast.

☆☆☆

(167)

Heri taba vimalamukhabhati dur halo gahan dukharabi
Phutilo mana pran mamo charanlalase, dinu hridayakamalatal pati.
Taba nayanajyotikana lagi tarun rabikiran uthe jagi.
Nayan khuli visvajan vadan tuli chahilo taba darashaparashasukh magi
Gagantal magan halo subhro taba hasite
Uthilo phuti kata kusumapanti – heri taba vimalamukhabhati.
Dhwanita van vihagakalatane, geet sav dhaay taba pane.
Purva gagane jagat jagi uthi gahilo, purno sav taba rachita gaane.
Premaras pan kari gaan kari kanane
Uthilo mana pran mama mati – heri tava vimalamukhabhati.

Beholding thy clean lustre of countenance the dense night of sorrow
is over
My mind and life rushed towards thy feet, I spread the
bunches of lotuses of my heart
With the touch of the light of thy eyes the young sunlight
wakes up
Opening the eyes and lifting the countenance the people of
the world looked up praying for
the touch of happiness of seeing thee
The sky is rapt with thy bright laughter
Innumerable buds of flowers blossomed, beholding thy
clean lustre of countenance.
With raptures of birds the forest is resounded,
all songs rush towards thee.
The world in the east awake and mused, with thy song
everything is filled in
The juices of love do I drink and sing in the garden
of flowers.
My mind and life are intoxicated, beholding thy
clean lustre of countenance.

☆☆☆

(168)

Ami sangsare mon diyechhinu, tumi apni se mon niyechho.
Ami sukh vale dukh cheyechhinu, tumi dukh vale sukh diyechho.
Hriday jahar satakhane chhilo sata swarther sadhane
Tahare kemoni kuraye anile, vandhile bhaktivandhane.
Sukh sukh kare dware dware more kata dike kata khonjale,
Tumi je amar kata aponar ebar se katha kojhale –
Karuna tomar kon path diye kotha nie jaay kahare --
Sahasa dekhinu nayan meliye
Enechho tomari duare.

I was attentive to the family, thou hast thyself taken away
that mind
I wanted sorrow as happiness, thou hast given happiness
as sorrow.
One whose heart was everywhere in performing numerous ends
How didst thou pick him up and bind him in the string
of devotion?
Thou hast made me unendingly seek in many directions from door to
door in the hope of happiness
How endearing thou art to me is made to be understood now
Thy pity takes one along the path somewhere none knows
Suddenly did I behold by opening the eyes
Thou hast brought me at thy door.

☆☆☆

INDEX OF FIRST WORDS : A

INDEX OF FIRST WORDS : 'B' **Page No.**